GENESIS

Foundations of Grace

VOLUME ONE | A STUDY OF GENESIS 1-11

JOANNA KIMBREL

Study Suggestions

We believe that the Bible is true, trustworthy, and timeless, and that it is vitally important for all believers. These study suggestions are intended to help you more effectively study Scripture as you seek to know and love God through His Word.

SUGGESTED STUDY TOOLS

- A Bible

- A double-spaced, printed copy of the book of the Bible that this study covers. You can use a website like *www.biblegateway.com* to copy the text of a passage and print out a double-spaced copy to be able to mark on easily.

- A journal to write notes or prayers

- Pens, colored pencils, and highlighters

- A dictionary to look up unfamiliar words

BEFORE YOU BEGIN

- Look into the context of the book of the Bible that you are studying, including the author, audience, cultural climate, genre, and purpose of the book. Consider where it fits in the biblical timeline.

- Read the book from start to finish at least once to gain a sense of the overall flow and argument of the book.

HOW TO USE THIS STUDY

Begin your study time in prayer. Ask God to reveal Himself to you, to help you understand what you are reading, and to transform you with His Word (Psalm 119:18).

Before you read what is written in each day of the study itself, read the assigned passages of Scripture for that day. Use your double-spaced copy to circle, underline, highlight, draw arrows, and mark in any way you would like to help you dig deeper as you work through a passage.

Try answering the questions provided at the end of a study day before reading the content that is written in the study.

Read the daily written content provided for the current study day.

Return to the questions that appear at the end of each study. Answer any that you were unable to complete and make any changes or additions based on what you have learned.

The inductive method provides tools for deeper and more intentional Bible study. To study a book of the Bible inductively, work through the steps below after reading background information on the book.

1 OBSERVATION & COMPREHENSION
Key question: What does the text say?

After reading the book of the Bible in its entirety at least once, begin working with smaller portions of the book. Read a passage of Scripture repetitively, and then mark the following items in the text:

- Key or repeated words and ideas
- Key themes
- Transition words (*Ex: therefore, but, because, if/then, likewise, etc.*)
- Lists
- Comparisons & Contrasts
- Commands
- Unfamiliar Words (look these up in a dictionary)
- Questions you have about the text

2 INTERPRETATION
Key question: What does the text mean?

Once you have annotated the text, work through the following steps to help you interpret its meaning:

- Read the passage in other versions for a better understanding of the text.
- Read cross-references to help interpret Scripture with Scripture.
- Paraphrase or summarize the passage to check for understanding.
- Identify how the text reflects the metanarrative of Scripture, which is the story of creation, fall, redemption, and restoration.
- Read trustworthy commentaries if you need further insight into the meaning of the passage.

3 APPLICATION

Key Question: How should the truth of this passage change me?

Bible study is not merely an intellectual pursuit. The truths about God, ourselves, and the gospel that we discover in Scripture should produce transformation in our hearts and lives. Answer the following questions as you consider what you have learned in your study:

- What attributes of God's character are revealed in the passage?

    Consider places where the text directly states the character of God, as well as how His character is revealed through His words and actions.

- What do I learn about myself in light of who God is?

    Consider how you fall short of God's character, how the text reveals your sin nature, and what it says about your new identity in Christ.

- How should this truth change me?

    A passage of Scripture may contain direct commands telling us what to do or warnings about sins to avoid in order to help us grow in holiness. Other times our application flows out of seeing ourselves in light of God's character. As we pray and reflect on how God is calling us to change in light of His Word, we should be asking questions like, "How should I pray for God to change my heart?" and "What practical steps can I take toward cultivating habits of holiness?"

ATTRIBUTES OF GOD

ETERNAL

God has no beginning and no end. He always was, always is, and always will be.

HAB 1:12 / REV. 1:8 / IS. 41:4

FAITHFUL

God is incapable of anything but fidelity. He is loyally devoted to His plan and purpose.

2 TIM. 2:13 / DEUT. 7:9
HEB. 10:23

GLORIOUS

God is ultimately beautiful, deserving of all praise and honor.

REV. 19:1 / PS. 104:1
EX. 40:34-35

GOOD

God is pure; there is no defilement in Him. He is unable to sin, and all He does is good.

GEN. 1:31 / PS. 34:8 / PS. 107:1

GRACIOUS

God is kind, giving to us gifts and benefits which we are undeserving of.

2 KINGS 13:23 / PS. 145:8
IS. 30:18

HOLY

God is undefiled and unable to be in the presence of defilement. He is sacred and set-apart.

REV. 4:8 / LEV. 19:2 / HAB. 1:13

IMMUTABLE

God does not change. He is the same yesterday, today, and tomorrow.

1 SAM. 15:29 / ROM. 11:29
JAMES 1:17

JEALOUS

God is desirous of receiving the praise and affection He rightly deserves.

EX. 20:5 / DEUT. 4:23-24
JOSH. 24:19

JUST

God governs in perfect justice. He acts in accordance with justice. In Him there is no wrongdoing or dishonesty.

IS. 61:8 / DEUT. 32:4 / PS. 146:7-9

LOVE

God is eternally, enduringly, steadfastly loving and affectionate. He does not forsake or betray His covenant love.

JN. 3:16 / EPH. 2:4-5 / 1 JN. 4:16

MERCIFUL

God is compassionate, withholding us from the wrath that we are deserving of.

TITUS 3:5 / PS. 25:10
LAM. 3:22-23

OMNIPOTENT

God is all-powerful; His strength is unlimited.

MAT. 19:26 / JOB 42:1-2
JER. 32:27

OMNIPRESENT

God is everywhere; His presence is near and permeating.

PROV. 15:3 / PS. 139:7-10
JER. 23:23-24

OMNISCIENT

God is all-knowing; there is nothing unknown to Him.

PS. 147:4 / I JN. 3:20
HEB. 4:13

PATIENT

God is long-suffering and enduring. He gives ample opportunity for people to turn toward Him.

ROM. 2:4 / 2 PET. 3:9 / PS. 86:15

RIGHTEOUS

God is blameless and upright. There is no wrong found in Him.

PS. 119:137 / JER. 12:1
REV. 15:3

SOVEREIGN

God governs over all things; He is in complete control.

COL. 1:17 / PS. 24:1-2
1 CHRON. 29:11-12

TRUE

God is our measurement of what is fact. By Him are we able to discern true and false.

JN. 3:33 / ROM. 1:25 / JN. 14:6

WISE

God is infinitely knowledgeable and is judicious with His knowledge.

IS. 46:9-10 / IS. 55:9 / PROV. 3:19

Creation

In the beginning, God created the universe. He made the world and everything in it. He created humans in His own image to be His representatives on the earth.

Fall

The first humans, Adam and Eve, disobeyed God by eating from the fruit of the Tree of Knowledge of Good and Evil. Because of sin, the world was cursed. The punishment for sin is death, and because of Adam's original sin, all humans are sinful and condemned to death.

Redemption

God sent his Son to become a human and redeem His people. Jesus Christ lived a sinless life but died on the cross to pay the penalty for sin. He resurrected from the dead and ascended into heaven. All who put their faith in Jesus are saved from death and freely receive the gift of eternal life.

Restoration

One day, Jesus Christ will return again and restore all that sin destroyed. He will usher in a new heaven and new earth where all who trust in Him will live eternally with glorified bodies in the presence of God.

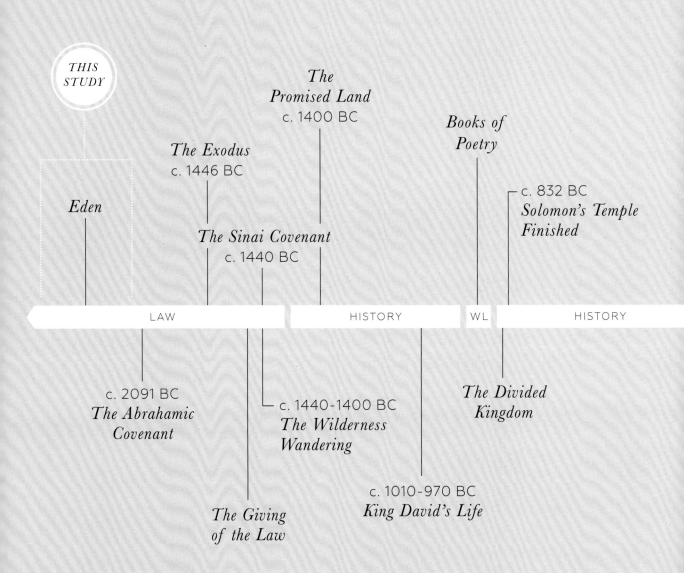

THIS STUDY

The Promised Land
c. 1400 BC

Books of Poetry

The Exodus
c. 1446 BC

c. 832 BC
Solomon's Temple Finished

Eden

The Sinai Covenant
c. 1440 BC

LAW · HISTORY · WL · HISTORY

c. 2091 BC
The Abrahamic Covenant

c. 1440-1400 BC
The Wilderness Wandering

The Divided Kingdom

c. 1010-970 BC
King David's Life

The Giving of the Law

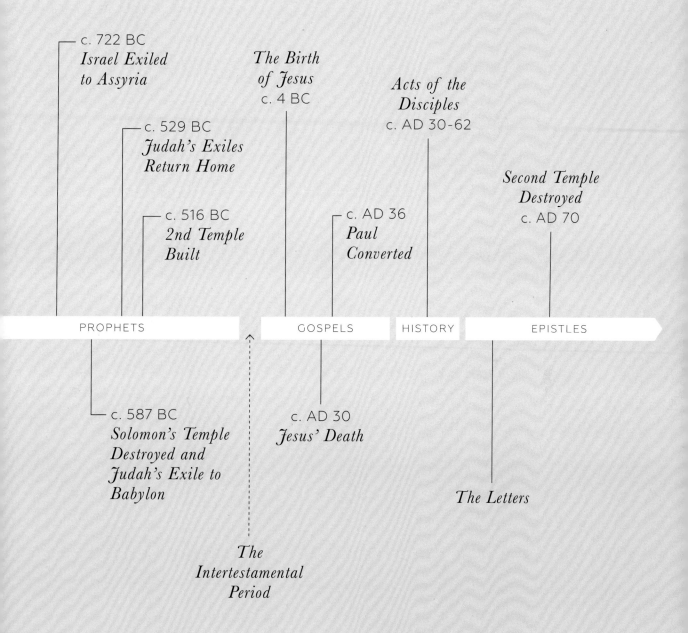

c. 722 BC
*Israel Exiled
to Assyria*

*The Birth
of Jesus*
c. 4 BC

*Acts of the
Disciples*
c. AD 30-62

c. 529 BC
*Judah's Exiles
Return Home*

*Second Temple
Destroyed*
c. AD 70

c. 516 BC
*2nd Temple
Built*

c. AD 36
*Paul
Converted*

PROPHETS GOSPELS HISTORY EPISTLES

c. 587 BC
*Solomon's Temple
Destroyed and
Judah's Exile to
Babylon*

c. AD 30
Jesus' Death

The Letters

*The
Intertestamental
Period*

Introduction *to* Genesis

Introduction to Genesis

"Genesis recounts the beginning of a story that God has been writing for all of history."

Genesis means beginning. The genesis of something is its creation, its origin, or its starting point. And so, the book of Genesis is a book of origins. Fittingly, Genesis is the very first book in the Bible, opening with God forming the universe by the word of His mouth, but this book of beginnings is about far more than the beginning of creation. Genesis recounts the beginning of a story that God has been writing for all of history. It is the beginning of a plan that has been in place since before God uttered the first, "Let there be." The book of Genesis depicts the beginning of planets and stars, oceans and rivers, insects and animals, but it is also the origin of God's image bearers and their covenant relationship with Him. It is the origin of human sin and the first promises of salvation. It is the beginning of a story of redemption, spanning from Genesis to Revelation. Genesis is the foundation of our understanding of God, humanity, sin, and salvation. It is the beginning of the story of God's people, which means it is the beginning of our story.

Genesis is not only the first book of the Bible but also part of a smaller portion of Scripture called the Pentateuch, which includes Genesis, Exodus, Leviticus, Numbers, and Deuteronomy. These first five books of the Bible are also called the Torah, which is the Hebrew term for the Law. Traditionally, these books have been attributed to Moses. Although there has been much debate over its authorship, the consensus among most evangelical scholars is that Moses is the primary author, with some additions and revisions by later contributors who provided updated city names and the account of Moses' death. There are multiple places where both the Old Testament and the New Testament assume Mosaic authorship, and most importantly, Jesus Himself mentions Moses as the author in John 5:45-46.

Moses likely wrote the book of Genesis to the Israelites in the late 15th century BC, during or shortly after their exodus in the wilderness. The Israelites had been enslaved in

Egypt for hundreds of years, living in a country worshiping false gods of the sun, moon, stars, and many other aspects of creation. In light of this recent history, Genesis opposes the polytheism of Egypt and much of the Ancient Near Eastern world by presenting a monotheistic God who rules over all of creation.

Genesis is essentially an introduction to the Pentateuch, the Old Testament, and the Bible as a whole, but Genesis is also the beginning of a much bigger story. It is a story of God's work of creation, the sin that brought about the fall of man and the world he inhabits, God's plan to redeem fallen sinners through Christ and make them His own, and the promise of a restored, new creation where the kingdom of heaven will be consummated. The purpose of this book of Genesis lays the foundation for that story, and as such, there is a lot that the book intentionally omits. Overall, Genesis is written in the style of a historical narrative, recording historical events in chronological order, although it contains other types and genres of literature throughout. Genesis leaves many questions unanswered, such as the particularities and mechanics of creation. This is not because the Bible is anti-science but because it is seeking to answer different questions. The Bible was never meant to be a science textbook, nor does it conflict with science. Its lack of scientific detail is a reflection of its purpose: to reveal the character of God and His story of redemption.

> Its lack of scientific detail is a reflection of its purpose: to reveal the character of God and His story of redemption.

The book of Genesis can be divided into two unequal parts. Chapters 1-11 consist of primeval history, covering the creation of the world and its history before Abraham, and chapters 12-50 recount the history of the patriarchs. This volume covers chapters 1-11. The storyline is driven by a family line. The book of Genesis is structured around genealogies, with each new section beginning with the same Hebrew word, *toledot*. This word is often translated as generations, family records, account, or descendants. *Toledot* is about family continuing on through time. Each new section of Genesis begins with "these are the generations, the descendants, the family records—of..." God makes a promise to Adam and Eve in Genesis 3 that He would give them an offspring who would undo the curse of sin, redeeming God's people from death and restoring all of creation—a promise that will ultimately find its fulfillment in Jesus Christ. Each new name in the *toledot* brings the hope that the offspring would arrive at last, but their failures point forward to the only One who would perfectly fulfill God's promise. The structure of Genesis shows God carrying His plan and promises through generation after generation, passed on from one person to the next, until each promise is fulfilled in the promised offspring, Jesus Christ.

The book of Genesis is a story of creation and recreation. It is a story of a good God and a world filled with sin. All of Genesis, and indeed all of the Old Testament, is waiting for the offspring promised to Adam who would restore what sin destroyed. All of Scripture points to Christ and the good news that He became a curse in order to bring a blessing. All of Scripture points to the gospel. Genesis is a book of beginnings, but from the very first words it points to the end, and we cannot properly understand the gospel without Genesis. Genesis marks the beginning of the greatest story ever told—a story whose end remains yet to be fulfilled, a story that we are living right now. God has graciously revealed to us the beginning and the end of the story in His Word, which we need in order to remain faithful and hopeful in the present.

Genesis marks the beginning of the greatest story ever told—a story whose end remains yet to be fulfilled, a story that we are living right now.

TOLEDOT

תּוֹלְדוֹת

Strong's H8435: (plural only) descent, i.e. family;
(figuratively) history: birth, generations.

THESE ARE THE TOLEDOT OF...

Primeval History

The heavens and the earth (2:4-4:26)

Adam (5:1-6:8)

Noah (6:9-9:29)

The sons of Noah (10:1-11:9)

Shem (11:10-26)

Patriarchal History

Terah (11:27-25:11)

Ishmael (25:12-18)

Isaac (25:19-35:29)

Esau (36:1-37:1)

Jacob (37:2-50:26)

TODAY'S QUESTIONS

What key words and themes did you notice in Genesis 1-11?

_____

_____

_____

_____

_____

_____

What did you observe about God's character in Genesis 1-11?

_____

_____

_____

_____

_____

_____

Write a prayer asking God to reveal Himself and transform your heart through the study of Genesis.

_____

_____

_____

_____

_____

_____

_____

_____

_____

_____

In the Begin-ning

For further study: Psalm 19:1-6, Psalm 90:2, Job 38-39, Isaiah 40:25-26, Isaiah 45:18, Romans 11:36

In the Beginning

"Before anything else existed, God was there."

The book of Genesis begins with God. "In the beginning God created the heavens and the earth." The subject of the first verse is the Hebrew word *Elohim*, which means God. This subject is carried throughout the rest of the chapter as it appears 32 times in just 31 verses. Such an opening verse is fitting because God is not only the subject of this chapter but also of the whole book of Genesis. These very first words of Scripture point us to the subject of the entirety of Scripture—God. From beginning to end, the Word of God reveals the character and works of God. It is all about Him. Genesis 1:1 discloses crucial information about who God is, and it is this truth that serves as the foundation of the entire Bible. Genesis 1:1 proclaims that there is one true God who is over all of creation. This verse contains only seven words in the original Hebrew, but it is brimming with truth about God's character.

Before anything else existed, God was there. No one created Him. He is completely self-existent. This aspect of God's character is known as His aseity. He depends on nothing and no one for anything, not even His own existence—He has everything He needs in Himself. He is totally self-sufficient. There is no one else in all of history who can claim this characteristic. Everything and everyone aside from God depends on Him for "life and breath and all things" (Acts 17:25).

God is also eternal. He has no beginning and no end. He was there in the beginning—the beginning of time, the beginning of creation—and He will be forever. He sees and knows the past, present, and future, inhabiting them all and not constrained by time's passing. He is outside of time but works in it as recorded in His Word and in ways that we cannot see. God is not surprised by anything, nor is He anxious about what is to come, because He works all things according to His will (Ephesians 1:11).

The God, who was there in the beginning, is the creator of all things. When Moses says, "God created the heavens and the earth," he is probably not referring to heaven in the sense of the place where God dwells, but more likely he is speaking of the place that is full of heavenly bodies—the sun and the moon, planets, stars, and galaxies. The primary audience of Genesis consisted of the Israelites who had been freed from centuries of slavery in Egypt, and the Egyptians were a polytheistic people who worshiped elements of creation as gods. Moses, therefore, is emphasizing that there are not many gods of the heavens and the earth—gods of the sun and stars and rivers and earth—but that there is one true God who created them all and is Lord over them all. Moreover, God is the only one capable of this kind of creative work. The Hebrew word for created in this verse is *bara*, and it is used in the Old Testament exclusively with God as its subject.

The description of God creating the heavens and the earth does not limit the scope of His creative work. This construction is a literary device called a merism, in which two opposite extremes represent the whole. To say that God created the heavens and the earth is also to say that He created everything in between. Genesis 1:1 unequivocally states that God made everything. From the microscopic world of atoms, bacteria, and DNA, to the hundreds of billions of galaxies in the observable universe, each thousands of light-years in size, God created all of it. Whether cells or black holes, from the tiniest particles to the unfathomable enormity of space, God made every bit. All of creation finds its origin in Him.

> He knows the end from the beginning. He would enter into this world that He created and suffer to save it. He would draw near to us, not out of obligation, but out of love, becoming human to die in our place.

This verse is just the beginning of a beautiful story that was in God's heart and mind long before He created the universe. He knows the end from the beginning. He would enter into this world that He created and suffer to save it. He would draw near to us, not out of obligation, but out of love, becoming human to die in our place. God owes nothing to us, but He cares for us and gave His own Son to save us. Even as God spoke the planets into existence, He knew how many hairs would be on your head at this very moment.

How should we respond to a God who is so great, who transcends above all, who is the Creator of all, and who rules over all? We respond in awe and worship to the greatness of the one true God. We rejoice as we see the work of His hands and join with all creation in declaring His glory. We throw aside all the gods we have made from created things and wholeheartedly turn to the Creator and serve Him only. It is our duty to worship the only One who has always been, but it is also our delight to draw near to the One who draws near to us in love. There is joy in depending on the only One who depends on nothing. He has everything we need. We should seek Him alone, and we find Him here in His Word.

This first verse of Genesis reveals much of God's character, but there is so much more of Him to be found in the treasure stores of His Word. As we continue through the book of Genesis, we will see the character of God progressively uncovered, and the knowledge of who He is that we will gain from this book is the foundation for a lifetime of glorious discovery in every page of Scripture.

It is our duty to worship the only One who has always been, but it is also our delight to draw near to the One who draws near to us in love.

TODAY'S QUESTIONS

Read Acts 17:22–29. What does Paul point out about God's character based on the truth of Genesis 1:1, and what does he say the response should be to that truth?

That he is the creator of all things and he needs nothing. That we should seek the Lord, that he is not far from us.

What created things do you tend to worship by making them the object of your hope or satisfaction? Some examples could include another person, money, a certain lifestyle, etc.

a clean house, a clean car

Go outside or look out a window, and look at the nature you can see around you. Take a few minutes to meditate on Genesis 1:1, and think about the fact that God created all of these things. Write a prayer of adoration and worship to Him.

Lord, Thank you for your creation the sunrise, the trees, the birds. If you hadn't created such things our world would be bland. Thank you for your creations.
Amen

Let There *Be*

Let There Be

"The earth was formless and empty, but God brought form and fullness."

The first words of the Bible revealed that the self-existing, eternal, one true God is the source of every created thing, and in the verses that follow, the story of creation unfolds. Verse 2 introduces a new character—the Spirit of God. From its opening verses the Bible presents a trinitarian God—a God who is three in one. The Trinity consists of three persons—the Father, the Son, and the Holy Spirit—who are all one essence. Each person of the Trinity exists simultaneously; each is distinct yet perfectly united. All three are fully God, have existed eternally, and are active in the work of creation. While this passage does not directly state the Son's involvement in creation, other passages of Scripture make it clear. John 1:1-3 shows that the Son is the Word of God through whom all things were made, and Psalm 33:6 indicates the involvement of the Father, Son, and Spirit. The members of the Trinity are united to each other in perfect love and perfect community, and it is out of the overflow of that love, not out of loneliness or need, that God creates.

Verse 2 reveals that at the beginning of creation, the substance that God brought into existence was "formless and empty." In Hebrew this phrase is *tohu wa-bohu*, a rhyming construction appearing frequently throughout the Old Testament, carrying the meaning of chaos, disorder, and non-functionality. The earth was unorganized and uninhabited, but the Spirit of God was hovering over the face of the waters like a mother bird hovering over her nest (Deuteronomy 32:11). This imagery indicates that the earth would not be formless and empty for long. The power of God was hovering—drawing near, nurturing, guiding—and something big was about to happen.

The earth was formless and empty, but God brought form and fullness. God brings order out of chaos. He brings purpose to what seems meaningless. Genesis 1 is filled with rhythmic repetition, highlighting the orderliness and intentionality of creation and revealing much about God's character. The predictable repetition of "let there be" and "it was so" emphasizes the creative power and authority of God in creating *ex nihilo*—out of nothing—while the refrain, "evening came and then morning," highlights the purposeful structure woven into creation. The methodical repetition of the chapter as a whole reflects the God who is its subject—He is a God of order.

The account of the six days of creation follows a parallel structure in which God brings form on days one through three and corresponding fullness on days four through six. In the first three days of creation, God forms, divides, and organizes, and on the subsequent days He fills what He has formed. Not only does God bring order from chaos, but He creates something out of nothing by the word of His mouth. Where there was darkness and disorder, God said, "Let there be light," and light came to be. On the first day God brought order to light and darkness, creating day and night, and on the corresponding fourth day He filled the heavens with lights—the sun, moon, and stars—to bring order to days and nights and times and seasons. Where God created the sky on the second day to separate the waters on the earth from the waters that would rain down from above, He filled the water and sky with creatures that swim and fly on the fifth day. On the third day God gathered up the waters and created dry land and the plants that grow on it, and on the sixth day God filled the earth with all the creatures that inhabit it. God brought order to disorder. Where there was emptiness and darkness, God filled and illuminated.

> Not only does God bring order from chaos, but He creates something out of nothing by the word of His mouth.

This passage of Scripture is the subject of much debate among believers. While some Christian scholars believe that the six days of creation represent six literal 24-hour periods, others believe that each day corresponds to an age in history. When approaching this chapter, it is important to recognize that the author's goal is not to recount all the details of the creation process or the exact method by which God made the universe. Whether the earth is thousands of years old or billions of years old is not a primary issue of Christian belief, and it should not be used as a litmus test to determine the orthodoxy, or right belief, of someone's faith. Well-studied believers with strong convictions about being faithful to the authority of Scripture have come to different conclusions about the details of how creation may have played out. What is of primary importance, however, is that God created the entire universe out of nothing, and He is the source of all things.

God is still in the business of bringing order from chaos and shining light in the darkness. Just as the word that God spoke produced light, God has sent His Son, who is the Word, to be the light of the world. Our hearts have been darkened by sin, but Jesus Christ brings light and life. The God who created the universe from nothing is able to produce faith where there is none. God speaks, and life springs forth.

As we look at the world around us, we can be overwhelmed by the chaos and disorder that we observe. Darkness and disorder seem to prevail, and seemingly endless striving and suffering can leave us feeling as if life is random and meaningless, but God brings purpose and fullness. The void within can feel even darker than the disorder around us, but we do not have to settle for emptiness, because satisfaction is found in Christ. When our sinful desires are out of control, God orders them and aligns them to His. When our anxious thoughts bounce around chaotically in our heads, the Word of God separates the truth from the lies. The Lord of the universe is the Lord of our hearts, and a life of longing finds fullness in Him. We find purpose in our maker.

God is still in the business of bringing order from chaos and shining light in the darkness.

TOHU WA-BOHU
Formless & Empty

Tohu Wa-Bohu describes the state of existence before creation. The earth was formless and empty (Genesis 1:2). In contrast, the six days of creation bring about form and fullness.

The first three days and the last three days run parallel to one another—days one through three showing form and days four through six showing fullness.

Let There Be

DAY 1

Night & Day

Separated light from darkness

DAY 2

Sky

Separated the waters

DAY 3

Earth & Seas

Gathered the waters

Sun
&
Moon

Sea Creatures
&
Winged Creatures

Land Creatures
&
Man

DAY 4

DAY 5

DAY 6

TODAY'S QUESTIONS

What does today's passage reveal about God's character?

That he likes and wants things in order. He brings an end to chaos.

How does the creation narrative impact the way you view the world around you?

It makes me appreciate the things in the world a lot more.

God is the one who brings form and fullness, but we often turn to other things for a sense of purpose or satisfaction. Where have you looked to bring form and fullness to your own life?

To my phone, friends or family. Sometimes even my work or food

Made in the Image of God

For further study: Colossians 1:15, Colossians 2:9, Hebrews 1:3, 1 Timothy 3:16

Made in the Image of God

"We were created to bear God's image."

God created the universe and formed and filled the earth with good and beautiful things, and now, half way through the final day of creation, something new is coming. The narrative that has been rhythmic and predictable up to this point now breaks form, signaling that what is about to happen is significantly distinct from what has come before. Where the creative refrain from the mouth of God had been, "Let there be," He now declares, "Let us make." This shift from third person to first person plural indicates that there is something uniquely personal about the final creative act of this narrative. In His crowning act of all creation, God created humans. Throughout Genesis 1, God declared after every element of creation that what He made was good, but after He brings man into existence, it is very good. So special among all of creation is man that the normal, linguistic pattern of the narrative is interrupted to express the exceptional beauty of this statement with poetic language and form. But what is so special about man? What distinguishes humans from the fish and birds and all the animals on the ground? Why is humanity designated as very good? Because they reflect the One who is perfectly good.

Humans are made in the image of God, the imago dei. As a child resembles his or her biological father, humans in a sense look like God, not in a physical sense of hair color or body type, since God is spirit, but in nature and character. All created things point to the character of the Creator, but humanity is unique in that we bear God's very image. God's image in us is evident in our ability to employ logic and reason and to form complex philosophical and theological thoughts. It manifests itself in the full range of emotions that we experience and in our capacity to love, since God is love. When God made the first humans in His image, their wills and desires were aligned to His, and they delighted in what He called good. God created man, male and female, each distinct and perfectly complementary, united in their differences to more fully display the character of the God whose image they bear.

As His image bearers, God set humans as His representatives on earth. As such, God gave the first humans a command, often called the creation mandate or the cultural mandate, to be fruitful, to multiply, to fill the earth, and to subdue the earth. This is a call to be God's co-rulers on earth—His viceroys—imaging Him in the work that He does. Just as God formed the earth, He commands humans to subdue the earth, nurturing it, tending it, and bringing order from chaos as they cultivate the ground. Likewise, God's filling of the earth is mirrored in the command for man to be fruitful, multiply, and fill the earth with more image bearers. Finally, man reflects God who rules over all of creation in the call to rule over the animals. The God who created the universe with nothing but a word graciously invites us to join Him and commune with Him in His good work. Certainly Moses is correct in saying that God blessed the first humans in verse 28. He gave them not only the immeasurable blessing of life itself but the blessing of the earth's abundance to sustain the life He gave and the sacred role of filling and tending to and ruling over everything God had made. Such a call is a gift of grace indeed.

> Rather than reflecting the goodness of God, our sinful thoughts and actions misrepresent His character.

While we were created to bear God's image and be His representatives in the world, the sad reality is that we fall terribly short of this calling. Rather than reflecting the goodness of God, our sinful thoughts and actions misrepresent His character. Sin has marred the image of God in us, but there is a better image bearer. Jesus Christ is the express image of God, the perfect imprint of His nature, the fullness of God who became man (Hebrews 1:3). Though we fail to accurately depict the goodness of God, we can look to Christ who is one with the Father and images Him perfectly, because He has revealed the Father to us. Sin has distorted the image of God in us, but as we gaze upon Christ, we can delight in His goodness still, rejoicing in the sure hope that to be united to Christ is to be conformed back to His image little by little, until He returns and the image of God in us is fully restored at last.

Though the image of God in us is distorted, it is not lost. Even after the fall, every human bears the image of God, clouded and warped though it may be, and therefore, every human life is sacred. Our worth comes not from accomplishments, appearance, or socio-economic status but from our status as image bearers of the holy God. Our value is not tied to what we have done or what has been done to us but what Christ has done for us. All people we encounter—regardless of their past, their skin color, or their beliefs, whether they treat you with kindness or hatred, from the unborn child to the elderly—all people are created in the image of God and should be treated with dignity, love, and respect. The imago dei means all human life is sacred. A sin against one who bears God's image is a sin against God Himself, and every single person is included in that category.

When God made the first humans, He blessed them, but soon the blessing would give way to a curse. Even so, the hope of blessing would not be lost. Time and time again, God's grace prevails to offer blessing to a people who deserve only the curse.

All people are created in the image of God and should be treated with dignity, love, and respect.

TODAY'S QUESTIONS

Read all of Genesis 1 aloud or listen to an audio Bible. What effect does the shift in language and literary style in today's passage have on the text? What does it reveal about the creation of man?

That God created everything and it was.
Man came and he blessed them, He
liked what he had done, when created man
all should be respected

Read Psalm 8. How does David respond to God creating man in His image and giving Him the creation mandate? How can you imitate David's attitude?

He praises him for all Creation.

Read James 3:7-10. What standard do you find yourself using to determine whether or not someone is worthy of your respect and kindness? What should be the determining factor?

I judge them by their character, from what I
may know about them.
God should be the determining factor, not
me, their words, even their attitude
towards certain things.

Divine Rest

For further study: Exodus 20:8-11, Deuteronomy 5:12-15, Matthew 11:28-30, Hebrews 4:1-11, Revelation 21

Divine Rest

> *"Like a painter who makes the final, perfectly placed brushstroke then sits back to admire His own work, God ceased from creating, satisfied and delighted in His work that was very good."*

At the end of the six days of forming and filling the earth, God rested from His work of creation. This rest is not a result of fatigue, as the all-powerful God has no need for restorative rest. The word translated "rest" here is the Hebrew word *shabath*, and it simply means cease. At the end of the sixth day, God shifted from declaring His creation "good" to calling it "very good," indicating that with the creation of His image bearers, creation was complete. Moreover, the number seven holds biblical significance as a number of completion. The repeated language of creating the heavens and the earth in Genesis 1:1 and 2:1 forms an inclusio, a literary device that uses corresponding language as bookends to indicate that everything in between is part of one section, and it is after the completion of this section that God rested. Like a painter who makes the final, perfectly placed brushstroke then sits back to admire His own work, God ceased from creating, satisfied and delighted in His work that was very good.

This seventh day is unique among the others, and the language and literary structure emphasizes its significance. The first three lines of verses 2 and 3 all repeat the language of the seventh day and God finishing, or resting, from the work he Had done in creation. This day contains no, "Let there be," or "Let us make," because God's work of creation was complete. It breaks the parallel pattern of the first six days to stand on its own. This day was blessed and declared to be holy, a day of joy and delight, consecrated and set apart for the Lord.

The concept of Sabbath continues throughout Scripture. In the book of Exodus, God freed His people from slavery in Egypt. God gave them the law, establishing them as a nation. In the Ten Commandments, God instituted the Sabbath, a day each week set apart from the others. After centuries of forced labor, God gave them a day of rest. This day that God blessed and declared holy is now a blessing to a weary people, a day commanded for them to rest from their labors and worship the One who is always working on their behalf. It is He who provides, sustains, and protects, and so they can rest as they trust in Him. This day was both a gift for the people of God and a day consecrated and set apart for the Lord. While it may seem contradictory to say that the Sabbath is for man and for God, these two realities are complementary. It is in the worship of God that true rest is found. Our joy is magnified when He is glorified.

The importance of the Sabbath carries on into the New Testament, our present reality, and ultimately into eternity. Through the Sabbath, the Hebrew people were given a taste of the greater rest to come. True Sabbath rest is ultimately found not in a day of the week but in Christ. While God rested from His work of creation when He completed it, Christ is seated on the throne, resting from His work of redemption. He completed this work as He breathed His last breath on the cross, uttering the words, "It is finished." Now Jesus invites us to come to Him, calling all who labor to find their rest in Him (Matthew 11:28-30). When we place our faith in Christ, we can cease from the need to work for our salvation and rest in the finished work of Christ. Believers are united to Jesus Christ in His work and His rest; His righteous work is given freely to us, and so we share also in His rest. We find rest from bearing the weight of our sin and shame because Christ bore it for us. We find rest from our fears in the sovereign hand of God who is for us. We find rest from the need to prove ourselves, perfect ourselves, or justify ourselves because our identity is wholly bound up in Jesus. Christ did not rest until redemption was accomplished, even to the point of dying for sinners like us, so now we can enter into His rest.

> Throughout all of Scripture, God is working to restore His presence to His people, and it is His presence that brings ultimate rest.

God's rest in Genesis 2 points forward to yet a greater rest. The concept of divine rest is closely tied to temple building, the place where God dwells. God's rest on the seventh day, along with many other elements of the creation account, indicate that God's purpose for creation is to make it a temple. God intends to make the earth His home. Throughout all of Scripture, God is working to restore His presence to His people, and it is His presence that brings ultimate rest.

In Christ, God Himself became a man and lived with us on the earth. We can experience Sabbath rest in Jesus today but only in part. We find rest for our souls as we trust in Jesus, but the rest we have in one sense we will experience in full when Christ returns again.

Jesus will usher in the new heaven and new earth, and the dwelling place of God will be fully and finally with us. When we live in the manifest presence of God, perfected and made new, we will be free from all sin, all pain, all weeping, and all mourning. On that day, we will enter our true and final Sabbath rest at last.

On this side of eternity, we can find rest in Christ in a wearied world. The degree to which we experience Sabbath rest directly correlates to our level of trust and dependence on Christ. Walking in obedience to Christ's call to abide in Him produces a richer and deeper rest as we pull not from our strength but His.

The description of the seventh day is missing the previous refrain, "And there was an evening, and there was a morning." This day of rest is a day without end, a reality of living in God's presence that will endure throughout all of eternity. Though sin corrupted God's design, we look forward to the day when the true Sabbath rest in the presence of God will be restored, and it will endure forever. We experience it now in part, but one day we will experience it in full—a day of true and lasting rest.

We can find rest in Christ in a wearied world.

TODAY'S QUESTIONS

What does God's rest reveal about what He has created?

That he is satisfied with his creation.
That it is ok to rest.

The Sabbath day was a day to rest and worship as the Israelites celebrated God's creation and redemption. Write a prayer of praise to God for what He has made and for how He has delivered you.

Thank you Lord for your creation of the earth. We see you in it everyday. Help me not to forget that if it wasn't for you we would not have the beauty of seeing you.

In what areas of yourself do you feel weary or burdened? What practical steps can you take to rest in Christ?

Right now I have a burden for my children that they will get right with God.

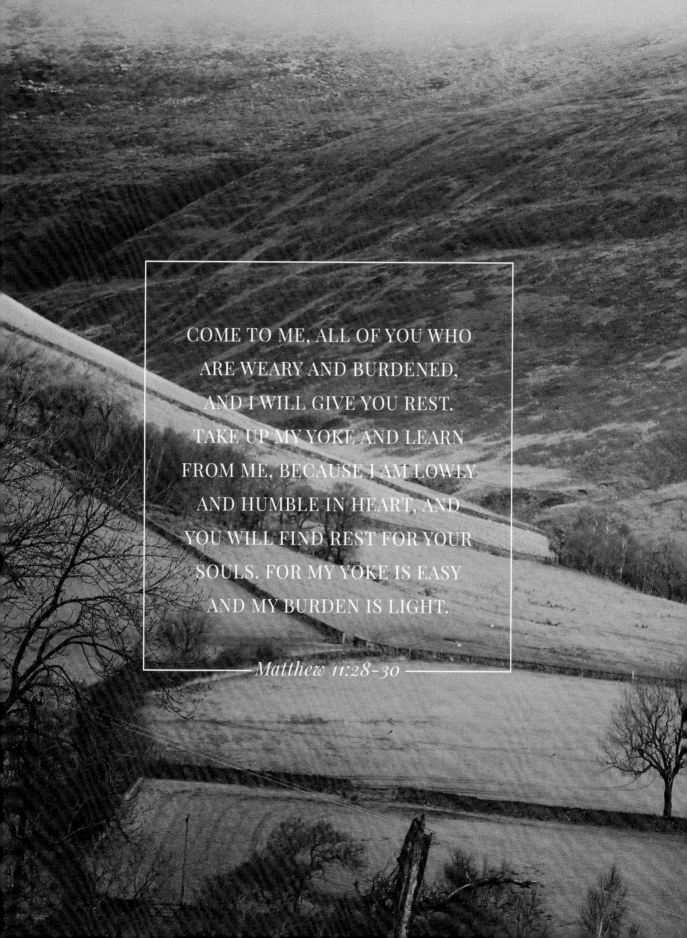

COME TO ME, ALL OF YOU WHO
ARE WEARY AND BURDENED,
AND I WILL GIVE YOU REST.
TAKE UP MY YOKE AND LEARN
FROM ME, BECAUSE I AM LOWLY
AND HUMBLE IN HEART, AND
YOU WILL FIND REST FOR YOUR
SOULS. FOR MY YOKE IS EASY
AND MY BURDEN IS LIGHT.

Matthew 11:28–30

SO GOD CREATED MAN IN HIS OWN IMAGE; HE CREATED HIM IN THE IMAGE OF GOD; HE CREATED THEM MALE AND FEMALE.

Genesis 1:27

Paraphrase the passage from this week.

God created the Earth in six days and on the 7th day he rested, because what he created was good.

What did you observe from this week's text about God and His character?

That he is an infinite God and what he created was good and he was pleased with it.

What does this week's passage reveal about the condition of mankind and about yourself?

_____
_____
_____
_____

How does this passage point to the gospel?

_____
_____
_____
_____

How should you respond to this passage? What is the personal application?

_____
_____
_____
_____

What specific action steps can you take this week to apply this passage?

_____
_____
_____
_____
_____

Living *in the* Garden— Temple

READ GENESIS 2:4-17

For further study: Exodus 25-28

Living in the Garden-Temple

"Yahweh Elohim is the creator God who is high above the cosmos yet draws near to dwell with His people."

Genesis 2:4 marks the beginning of a new section with the Hebrew *toledot*, announcing the records of the creation of the heavens and the earth. Everything that has come before today's passage can be viewed as an introduction, providing foundational information about the one true God of creation. In Genesis 2, Moses zooms in from the creation of the cosmos to the garden of Eden. This new section of Genesis focuses on the relationship between God and man. One significant element that contributes to this emphasis is the shift in the name used for God. All of Genesis leading up this point has used the title *Elohim* to refer to God, a name that underscores His creative work. Now the name that is repeated over and over again is *Yahweh Elohim,* The Lord God. *Yahweh* is God's covenant name and personal title. A covenant is a binding and deeply personal agreement. Covenants are the means through which God relates to His people. Through His covenant promises He brings about redemption. *Yahweh Elohim* is the creator God who is high above the cosmos yet draws near to dwell with His people.

Before God created man, the earth was untended. The lack of plants on the ground was likely due to the fact that man was not there to irrigate it. The text says that God "formed" the man out of the dust of the ground. The word "formed" carries a sense of intentionality. Like a potter who forms a lump of clay, God forms man with purposeful design and craftsman-like artistry. He took mere dust and produced an impossibly intricate creature whose cells, organs, and systems function in harmony together. How great is the mind of God to transform dirt into DNA, dust into flesh and blood! So closely connected to the earth, so deeply physical is man that the word for man in this passage (*ha adam*) is extremely similar to the word for ground (*ha adama*). But man is not merely physical. God breathed life into man, taking what is lowly and humble and forming it into His own image. So intimate and unique is the connection between God and man that God's own breath fills his lungs.

After God formed man, He placed him in a garden in Eden. The word "Eden" means delight, and the garden was bursting with provisions for man's enjoyment. Like a loving father, God set before man a luxurious paradise, filled with plants that were beautiful to behold and delicious to eat. The rivers that watered it created a lush landscape, and it was probably located in Mesopotamia, which means in the middle of rivers. Amidst all the bounty, the most wonderful thing about the garden was that God lived there. The parallels between the garden of Eden and the temple of the Old Testament indicate that Eden was in a sense the first temple, the archetype for future tabernacles and temples. The temple was the place where God dwelled, just as He dwelled in Eden. Like the temple, Eden's entrance was to the east. The language used to describe the man, Adam, characterizes him as the first priest. He was commanded to work the garden and watch over it. This language is specifically used to describe the service of the priest in the tabernacle and temple. The Tree of Life is like the lampstand outside the temple's holy of holies, and both the garden and the temple are described as containing precious jewels, gold, and onyx. Adam's call was to guard and take care of the garden-temple, the very dwelling place of God.

God related to the first man through a covenant, a binding agreement. The terms of the covenant included permissions and a prohibition. God gave man the abundance of the garden for his nourishment and pleasure. He gave him permission to partake of every tree in the garden except one. The prohibition was that man could not eat from the Tree of Knowledge of Good and Evil. This tree, along with the Tree of Life that would provide unending life, was at the garden's center. Man had no need to eat from this tree because he had access to all the knowledge and wisdom he needed in God Himself. To choose to eat from the tree would be to side-step God's design, to seek wisdom apart from Him, and to decide for himself what is right and wrong instead of trusting in the Lord. The punishment for disobeying the covenant's terms would be death. This covenant is called the covenant of works. If man honored the covenant, he would live, but if he disobeyed—if he sinned against God—the result would be death.

God's design from the very beginning has been to live among His people, but something went terribly wrong in the garden. Man would break the covenant, but God already had a plan. Even before He created the heavens and the earth, God made a

> To choose to eat from the tree would be to side-step God's design, to seek wisdom apart from Him, and to decide for himself what is right and wrong instead of trusting in the Lord.

plan to save sinful humans who would choose to rebel against Him. God had a plan to give the life of His own Son in exchange for the lives of those who would reject Him. Even if we do not know what is coming in chapter 3, all we have to do is look around the world to see that we do not live in the land of delight that is described here. Even so, the hope of Eden is not lost. Jesus Christ has come in the flesh to dwell with us, and He will come again to restore what was lost in Eden. He will come again to renew and restore the garden-temple at last.

God's design from the very beginning has been to live among His people.

TODAY'S QUESTIONS

What does God's design for the garden reveal about the way He cares for man?

That he wants the best for man,
he created was beautiful and had
given man everything he needs.

How does the description of Eden differ from your experience of the world today?

Eden is a beautiful place w/out sin,
unlike the world today, we live in a
very corrupt world w/ sin and uglyness
all around

How does the brokenness of this world cause you to long for the restoration of what was lost in Eden?

I can't wait to see the garden of
Eden, there will be so pretty and
the weather will be nice, not to
mention we get to see our loved ones.

At
Last

At Last

"Man and woman would be different yet the same — partners perfectly fashioned to complement one another and more fully display the image of God in His unity and diversity."

The rhythm of creation has been one of God speaking, creating, and deeming what He made to be good. Genesis 2:18 interrupts the repeated, "It was good," with a startling, "It is not good." This language in the Hebrew is very strong. There was something woefully missing from God's creation. What was the deficit that must be remedied? God declared, "It is not good for the man to be alone." The man created in God's image could not reflect God's plurality on his own. He was severely lacking. He needed another. So God resolved to make a helper for him. The term helper does not in any way imply inferiority. In fact, this same term is one that God uses to describe Himself as the helper of His people. The Hebrew text literally says God would make help as opposite to him. Man's helper would be a corresponding counterpart. Like puzzle pieces that fit perfectly together, she would provide what man lacked, and vice versa. Man and woman would be different yet the same — partners perfectly fashioned to complement one another and more fully display the image of God in His unity and diversity.

Adam became painfully aware of his own need as he named each creature God had made. God had named many elements of creation, calling day and night, earth and sea, times and seasons, by their names and so displaying His sovereign rule over it all. In naming the animals, Adam exercised his God-given role as co-ruler. Naming the animals was no simple task. The name of each animal would reflect something about its very nature. As Adam closely examined each creature, he became increasingly aware of the grievous reality that he was somehow alone. In all of the abundance of creation, Adam found not a single one who was like him. The animals were insufficient for companionship, unable to join him in the call to rule over the earth. Perhaps Adam was hopefully expectant as he observed the vastness of God's creation. Surely among the millions of species of animals there would be a helper for him, but creature after creature passed before him, and not a single one was like Adam. So God put Adam into a deep sleep and removed a rib bone from his side. Man was formed from dust, and woman was formed from man. They were made of the same substance. In biblical Hebrew, bone and flesh indicated a special kinship, much like the modern English way of describing people as sharing blood.

Adam awoke, and God brought the woman to him. In answer to the void that Adam experienced, God gave him the gift of one who is so like him that she was formed from his very bones. Adam's response is an eruption of joy. In the first human words recorded in Scripture, Adam broke forth into poetry. With the elation that comes from a deep longing fulfilled, Adam cried out, "at last!" In all the bounty of creation, not one was found who could be his equal until that moment. At last the one who was bone of his bone and flesh of his flesh had come! He had named all the creatures of the earth, and none of them matched his nature, but now he sees one like him and names her woman. He names her *isha*, woman, because she came from *ish*, man. Their names and their natures are alike. The magnificence of the woman was not merely that she was made of the same matter as Adam, for bones are just bones without the Spirit's breath to enliven them. The beauty of the woman is that she bore the same image as man. She too was made after God's likeness—at last, a fellow image bearer. As in Genesis 1:27, such a mysterious and glorious reality can only begin to be expressed through the emotional depth of poetry.

> In answer to the void that Adam experienced, God gave him the gift of one who is so like him that she was formed from his very bones.

This passage forms the foundation for biblical teaching on marriage. Jesus and the New Testament authors recognized this passage as God's institution of marriage. In verse 24, Moses indicates that this union is the model for marriage. Marriage is a sacred thing. God's design for marriage is that it is a binding relationship between one man and one woman. A man is to leave his family. This word does not describe a physical departure, as it was Jewish custom for a woman to come and live with her husband and his family. Rather, this statement is about loyalties. When a man marries a woman, his primary loyalty is to his wife. He is also called to cleave to his wife. This word has the sense of sticking together. He does not just hold on to his wife, but God binds them together. Marriage is meant to be permanent. So bound to one another are a husband and wife that God makes them one flesh. This union should never be taken lightly, but all who enter the marriage covenant should consider with solemnity the words of Christ in Matthew 19:6: "What God has joined together, let no one separate."

The description of the woman as man's helper makes clear the goal of marriage: joining together to do the work that God has called us to do. On this side of the cross, the New Testament gives us a fuller picture of marriage's purpose. Paul tells us in Ephesians 5 that marriage is meant to be a picture of Christ and the church. It should image the sacrificial love of Christ who gave Himself up for His church. It should be marked by helping one another to grow in holiness. Marriage should reflect the good news of the gospel to all those who see it.

It is not good for man to be alone. We were made for community, reflecting the unity and diversity of the Trinity together. This happens in marriage, but it also happens in the church as we are united to believers who, like us, are united to Christ. We may be tempted in reading this passage to think that someone's life is incomplete until and unless they marry, but we must remember the greater reality to which marriage points. The union of marriage is but a shadow of believers' union with Christ. Our greatest needs are not fulfilled in marriage but in Jesus. Jesus Himself even encourages singleness to those who are able. For the single person, you are not incomplete apart from a spouse. You are made whole in your union with Jesus. For the married person, your spouse can never bear the burden of fulfilling all your needs and desires. You must turn to Jesus.

Chapter 2 ends with the statement that the man and the woman were naked but felt no shame. In the background of this beautiful story of a joyous union looms the sorrow of brokenness. We know the shame that comes from being exposed. We are well acquainted with the need to cover up that accompanied vulnerability. The thought of being naked—whether physically, spiritually, or emotionally—without even the faintest hint of shame is unimaginable. The very mention of this shame-free reality is a painful reminder that something went terribly wrong. Indeed, the picture of shameless nakedness foreshadows the coming shame of sin.

We were made for community, reflecting the unity and diversity of the Trinity together.

TODAY'S QUESTIONS

According to God's design in Genesis 2, what should a healthy marriage relationship look like? How do you see the effects of sin on marriage?

A healthy marriage should have God at the very beginning of it. Man should leave his family to join w/ her, they work together

What does God's statement that it is not good for man to be alone tell you about the importance of godly community?

That we need someone to share it with, it is not good to be alone

How have you seen the tendency in your own life to place the burden of your happiness and identity on marriage, singleness, or some other human relationship? How is Christ our greater identity and satisfaction?

Christ is our greater identity because he supplies our needs and he is at the top of marriage. We find our identity in Christ.

The Deceiver and the Deceived

The Deceiver and the Deceived

"God had given them the abundance of the garden, but the serpent painted as stingy the boundary that God had given them for their good."

All was well in Eden. God had created the vast universe and within it a planet teaming with life, overflowing with fruitfulness and joy in the presence of the Lord God. God formed man and woman in His own image, and all of it was very good. However, this perfect reality would soon be corrupted, and chapter 3 begins with the introduction of one who came to sew distrust. The serpent who approached the woman is later identified as the devil in Revelation 20:2. While God speaks only words of truth, the devil is the "father of lies," and his deceitful speech overflows from his character (John 8:44).

The serpent's speech is careful and calculated. Chapter 2 had been employing the personal name for God, *Yahweh Elohim*, but the serpent created a sense of distance from God by using the impersonal *Elohim*. Perhaps the serpent meant to give the illusion that the woman could escape God's gaze and get away with disobedience. Where the first humans had nothing but complete trust in God, the serpent planted seeds of doubt with the words, "Did God really say?" In this simple phrase the devil implied that the word of God is subject to the critique of man, but it is God's words that are the authority on truth. The devil twisted the words of God, asking if God had really prohibited them from eating of any tree in the garden when His prohibition was only for one tree. God had given them the abundance of the garden, but the serpent painted as stingy the boundary that God had given them for their good.

The woman responded to the serpent, but even her correction was filled with subtle errors. She followed the serpent's lead in using the impersonal *Elohim*. R. Kent Hughes points out that the woman diminished, added to, and softened the word of God. God had told them that they could eat of every tree except one, but the woman left out the word, "every," diminishing the gracious generosity of God. She also added to God's words by saying that God forbade them not only from eating the fruit of the tree but also from touching it. This amendment to the words of God portrayed Him as overly strict and harsh. Finally, the woman softened God's words by removing the word "certainly" from His warning that if they ate the fruit of the tree, they would certainly die. By twisting the words of God, the serpent influenced Eve's own view of God as someone who wanted to withhold good things from her, who was overly harsh, and who would not follow through on the threat of judgment. The woman was primed for what would come next: the blatant denial of God's words.

In direct opposition to God's words, the devil declared, "You will not certainly die." In place of the good commands that God had set before Adam and Eve, Satan presented a false gospel. Eat the fruit, and you will be like God. Eat the fruit, and gain wisdom that He does not offer you. This is the thing that will satisfy you. Eat this fruit, and you will not need God. You will be your own god. The woman saw the appeal of the fruit and chose to believe the lies of Satan rather than the life-giving truth of God. In a tragically simple demise, she saw the fruit, took it, and ate. She gave some to her husband who had not been deceived (1 Timothy 2:14) but in a willful act of defiance, ate the forbidden fruit rather than obeying the words of God.

> In a moment, everything changed. The fruit that promised divinity turned to poison in their mouths.

The result of their disobedience reveals that the devil's lie came in the form of a half-truth. Their eyes were indeed opened as he promised, and for the first time, they knew evil. The devil had promised them that the fruit would make them like God, and in some small sense, it did. But their sin marred the image of God in them. The evil they came to know was their own sin. In a moment, everything changed. The fruit that promised divinity turned to poison in their mouths. Where they knew only goodness, they now became painfully acquainted with shame. Their sin was exposed, and they tried desperately to cover it up.

Because of the disobedience of our first parents, we have all inherited their sin, even from birth. We too know the shame that leaves us feeling exposed, and we attempt to cover it up or hide. On that sad day, our first parents took and ate, but years later Jesus would call us to take and eat of a better food. On the night before Jesus' death, He instituted the Lord's Supper. He gave His disciples bread and wine representing His body and blood given for the forgiveness of their sins on the cross. Jesus is the better Adam who offers us the food, not of sin and death, but of righteousness and life, and He calls us to "take and eat" (Matthew 26:26).

God has graciously given us His Word. He has revealed Himself to us and shown us the truth. We have everything we need for life and godliness in His Word (2 Peter 1:3), but the deceiver presents us with half-truths and lies everywhere we turn. He tries to lead us away from the truth by twisting the truth. He distorts the good character of God to make Him seem unloving, unjust, and dishonest, sewing distrust that primes our hearts to accept more obvious denials of God's Word. When competing voices tell us what we should believe and do, we must return to the voice of truth. In moments of deception, we must remind ourselves of God's good character. We must saturate ourselves in His Word and test everything against Scripture. The lies of the enemy bring only death and destruction, but God's Word brings abundant life.

His divine power has given us everything required for life and godliness through the knowledge of him who called us by his own glory and goodness.

—

2 Peter 1:3

TODAY'S QUESTIONS

Read 2 Corinthians 11:3-4. Eve believed the false gospel that there was wisdom and happiness to be found apart from God. What are some false gospels you are tempted to believe in your own life that look desirable but are contrary to God's Word?

gluttony when it comes to food

How do you see Eve's desire to be like God reflected in your own life?

wanting to see what things are all about and see if things will happen

The serpent denied God's judgment for sin, and many people today make the same claim. Why is the denial of judgment both enticing and harmful?

Because sin is made to look good, but when we take part we are disobeying god & God will punish us

What are some practical ways you can saturate yourself in the Word of God this week?

Study his word, listen to praise music talk w/ someone

A *Gracious* Confron- tation

A Gracious Confrontation

"God approached His wayward image bearers as a loving father approaches disobedient children."

The man and woman had sinned against God. The subsequent shame they experienced left them desperately longing to be covered, but their efforts to make sufficient clothing for themselves proved to be futile. Then they heard a familiar sound. The Lord was approaching. While the serpent and the woman referred to God only as the impersonal *Elohim*, the text once again employs *Yahweh Elohim*. The illusion that God was far off was now broken as the man and woman heard the sound of God walking in the garden. He came to them in the cool of the day when the air was pleasant and the breeze was sweet. On any other day, His approach would have been a delight. On this sorrowful day, their sin caused the man and woman to hide from God's presence. They were ashamed to be seen.

God approached His wayward image bearers as a loving father approaches disobedient children. He asked them questions even though He already knew the answers, calling them to recognize and admit their sin. He pursued them in their brokenness. He asked the man, "Where are you?" Like a parent who calls, "Where are you?" to a young child with a chocolate stained face who is hiding after taking cookies from the jar, God's question implies far more than physical location. It calls the man to reveal himself and the shameful state he has entered because of his disobedience. For the first time, fear entered the scene. Man had experienced only pleasure in God's presence, but now he was afraid. For a sinful person to be in the presence of a holy God is a fearful thing. His goodness requires that evil be destroyed. His justice demands blood for sin. God had warned of such an outcome when He told them that defying God's commands would lead to death.

Adam's response was not to reveal his sin but only his shame. He told the Lord that he hid and was afraid because he was naked. The Lord pressed in to draw out the man's sin by asking him how he knew he was naked. Shame is always connected to sin, whether it be a person's own sin or the result of being sinned against. So the Lord asked him if he had eaten from the tree of which God told him not to eat. God knew the answer, but God was inviting man into a conversation with Him. He was giving Adam the opportunity to own his sin and be honest before God. But instead, Adam attempted to minimize his wrongdoing. He pointed to the woman who gave him the fruit instead of recognizing that he should have submitted to God's instructions. The perfectly loving and harmonious union between the man and woman was now broken. Sin divided them. Moreover, he deferred his own responsibility by pointing a finger at God. He was the one who gave him the woman to begin with. The man denied God's good character by implying that God had tempted him. God's next question was for the woman. When the Lord questioned her, she too looked to another to bear the burden of responsibility as she pointed to the serpent who deceived her.

The warning of Genesis 2:17 that death would come as a result of disobedience might leave us surprised when Adam and Eve do not die immediately. He draws out their sin, calling them to see and confess it, not to humiliate them, but in order to restore them. The man and woman attempted to shift blame from themselves onto another, yet that sin and shame could never rest as a burden to be wholly borne by anyone but Christ. Our only hope to escape condemnation and take hold of life is Jesus Christ. He has borne our sin and shame, being utterly blameless yet receiving our punishment on our behalf. God is gracious to reveal to us our sin so that we might recognize our need for One who is sinless.

We, too, tend to minimize our sin. We cover it up. We blame our experiences and circumstances. Perhaps we try to hide from God for fear of His displeasure and judgment. But because of Christ, if we put our faith in Him, we do not have to fear God's wrath. There is freedom in confession because it leads to forgiveness. God intentionally worked to reveal to Adam and Eve their sin, and the Scripture that follows reveals that He did not intend to leave them without a rescuer. God is faithful to reveal our sin to us as well, using difficulties and hardships to show us our need for the Savior so that we might run to Him.

Our only hope to escape condemnation
and take hold of life is Jesus Christ.

TODAY'S QUESTIONS

According to James 1:13-15, what is the true source of our temptation?
What does God's dialogue with Adam and Eve reveal that they wrongly
believe about temptation?

They blamed God, or some one else for
their sin.
God did not tempt them.

Do you ever find yourself shifting the blame for your own sin?
Who or what do you blame?

Yes, sometimes it is the people we are
around that we blame

Read 1 John 1:9. Write a prayer confessing the ways you have been minimizing,
hiding, or denying your sin. Ask God to reveal any blind spots you may have.

Lord, I pray for forgiveness. If there is any
sin in my life I take full responsibility for
it. Help me to avoid it and turn to you
In that time. I pray you will remove anything
that is hindering my walk you.
Amen

A Curse and a Promise

A Curse and a Promise

*"God in His justice declared a curse that would extend to all
of humanity and to the ends of the earth."*

God's image bearers broke the covenant of works that God established. Covenants include blessings for obedience and curses for disobedience. The man and woman forfeited the blessing of everlasting, abundant life in God's presence when they chose to give in to temptation. Contrary to the lies of the serpent, God was true to His word to punish sin. The man and woman had not become their own gods but remained under the authority of *Yahweh Elohim*. God in His justice declared a curse that would extend to all of humanity and to the ends of the earth.

The Lord did not question the serpent but simply pronounced a curse upon him. The serpent would be the most cursed of all the animals. The language of eating dust emphasizes the snake's humiliation. He is unique among animals in that his curse will never be reversed. The serpent's curse extended beyond the physical animal to the devil himself. He will not prevail, but even as he inflicts harm, he will be destroyed. His head will be crushed.

God turned next to the woman. The curse of sin brought with it pain and sorrow. The woman would experience pain in bearing children. This pain certainly includes the physical agony of childbirth itself but also the emotional turmoil of raising children in a fallen world. Not only would the relationship between parents and children be damaged but so too would the marriage relationship. God had ordained that man would lead the woman, evidenced by the order in which He addressed them in His questioning. As a result of her sin, the woman would desire to exercise dominion over her husband and therefore step outside of the authority of God. Instead of a perfectly loving and harmonious union according to God's design, marriage would become a power struggle between sinful spouses trying to domineer over one another. Adam's curse extended beyond himself to the earth. Working the ground would no longer be an easy and joyful work. Thorns and thistles would make work that was once pleasant now painful. This passage gives a picture of a life marked by toil, pain, and hardship until it ends in death. The curse reached into every corner of creation. No square centimeter is untouched by sin.

Our first parents broke the covenant of works that God had set before them, and they therefore brought upon themselves the covenant curse. Covenants function with federal headship, which means that there is a single person who stands as a representative for everyone else who is under the covenant. This representative is called a covenant head, and what is true of the covenant head is true of those whom he represents. Adam is the covenant head for the covenant of works, and his failure passes on to us. Every human being has inherited the original sin of Adam. We are all born as fallen creatures in a fallen world. We who were made in God's image have twisted and distorted that image in us. Every single sin is an attack against the character of the God whom we were made to represent. Not one of us is without sin, and our sinfulness means that each one of us is condemned to death. It is a grievous thing that the world that God formed and filled with abundant life has been spoiled by rebellion. It is good to feel the sorrow of this reality. It is good to mourn over sin.

> Adam failed us when he transgressed the covenant, but we have a new covenant head in Jesus Christ.

In the midst of the curse, God made a promise. The devil would not prevail, but God would send One who would destroy him. The animal skins used to cover the nakedness of the man and woman point forward to the One who would give His own life to cover our shame and clothe us in righteousness. Adam failed us when he transgressed the covenant, but we have a new covenant head in Jesus Christ. He is the perfect Son of God who became a man and lived a life of perfect righteousness and obedience to God. Now we who place our faith in Him have Him as our representative. He succeeded where Adam failed, and His obedience is credited to us. What is true of Him is true of us. He paid the penalty for our sin in His own death, and He secured for us the blessing of eternal life in God's presence. He is the better Adam, the last Adam, who perfectly fulfilled the covenant of works on our behalf. In God's incredible grace, the woman is named Eve, meaning "the mother of all living." Life would spring forth from the woman who deserved only death. Indeed, her offspring would be the very giver of life. From her line would come the Savior.

God sent Adam and Eve out of the garden. He set two cherubim to guard its entrance, much like the two cherubim who would be at the entrance of the temple. The first man and woman were exiled from the garden-temple and from the dwelling place of God whose presence brings fullness of joy (Psalm 16:11). Throughout the rest of Scripture, God works to restore His presence to His people, not because we deserve it but because He loves us.

Adam and Eve sought happiness apart from God and His good commands, but only God can satisfy. The sorrow of the curse was an act, not only of God's judgment but also of His grace. God replaced joy with sorrow so that Adam and Eve would never lose sight of their true source of joy and their need for a savior. We too experience all kinds of sorrow and pain. We feel the effects of the curse in broken relationships, sickness and disease, and financial difficulties. We know what it is like to bear the shame of our past actions or the sinful actions of others who have hurt us. We feel the ache of loneliness. We grieve over injustice, hatred, and decay. We know the weariness that comes from battling sinful thoughts and attitudes that feel out of our control. We are well acquainted with the curse, but may our sorrow turn our hearts to the giver of joy. We have access to God's presence through Jesus Christ now, and we will experience His presence in full when Jesus comes again. May the curse always remind us of the promise, and may our pain lead us to run to the giver of life.

You reveal the path of life to me; in your presence is abundant joy; at your right hand are eternal pleasures.

—

Psalm 16:11

TODAY'S QUESTIONS

How do you see the effects of the fall in the world today?

drugs, alcohol, people fighting each other, families against each others,

How has your pain in your own life drawn you to Christ?

I want to see my loved ones, He can comfort me, during my pain

We are free to confess our sins to God and to grieve over them because Christ offers us forgiveness. Write a prayer confessing some specific sins to God.

Lord, I confess my sins to you. I know, I have had thoughts about others, may have talked about them, Lord I ask forgiveness, help me Lord to turn to you when I feel the need, help me to think positive about every situation, in Jesus name I pray,

BUT GOD PROVES HIS OWN
LOVE FOR US IN THAT WHILE
WE WERE STILL SINNERS,
CHRIST DIED FOR US. HOW
MUCH MORE THEN, SINCE WE
HAVE NOW BEEN JUSTIFIED BY
HIS BLOOD, WILL WE BE SAVED
THROUGH HIM FROM WRATH.

— *Romans 5:8-9* —

AND THE MAN SAID:
THIS ONE, AT LAST,
IS BONE OF MY BONE
AND FLESH OF MY
FLESH; THIS ONE
WILL BE CALLED
"WOMAN," FOR SHE
WAS TAKEN FROM MAN.

Genesis 2:23

WEEK TWO REFLECTION

Paraphrase the passage from this week.

_____

_____

_____

_____

_____

_____

_____

_____

_____

_____

_____

_____

What did you observe from this week's text about God and His character?

_____

_____

_____

_____

_____

_____

_____

What does this week's passage reveal about the condition of mankind and about yourself?

_____

_____

_____

_____

How does this passage point to the gospel?

_____

_____

_____

_____

How should you respond to this passage? What is the personal application?

_____

_____

_____

_____

What specific action steps can you take this week to apply this passage?

_____

_____

_____

_____

The First Gospel

The First Gospel

*"In justice, God pronounced judgment for sin, but His justice
would not be without mercy."*

God formed a beautiful and intricate world and filled it with goodness. He created people to bear His image, to live in His presence, and to reflect His work and character in the world. All was well, until man sinned. The image of God was egregiously marred when Adam and Eve rebelled against the holy God. With the fall of man came the curse of sin, bringing death and sorrow to man and the earth he inhabits. In justice, God pronounced judgment for sin, but His justice would not be without mercy. In the middle of the curse, God made a gracious promise.

In Genesis 3:15, God gave the first glimpse of the gospel. Theologians called this first the protoevangelium, which means the first gospel. The word "gospel" simply means good news. When the people God made out of love rejected Him, He offered them good news. When God cursed the serpent, He made a promise of an offspring who would make right what had gone terribly wrong. From Eve's line a seed would come who would destroy the devil. This savior would suffer, enduring the serpent's strike on His heel, but He would still have the final victory. He would crush the head of the serpent, inflicting a mortal wound that would put an end to the deceiver's reign. The protoevangelium is the promise of a savior who would rescue God's people from the death they inflicted upon themselves through sin. He would give life to those who merited death. God gives them the grace of hope in their hopelessness.

The first gospel gave a small glimpse into the beauty of God's grace, and over time He would increasingly reveal His plan to redeem His people. We have the incredible privilege of living on the other side of the cross. God has revealed the glory of the gospel to us in His Son, Jesus Christ. He is the promised offspring. He is the one who would crush the serpent's head. He is hope in our brokenness.

When Adam sinned that day, he passed on the curse to all of humanity. Every human, like Adam, has sinned against God. There is not a single person who is good on his or her own. We were made to bear God's image, but we have all fallen short of His glory. Because of our sin, we are condemned to death. Our sentence is not only a physical death, but we experience spiritual deadness as well. Apart from Christ, we are dead in our sins, walking in the ways of the devil that lead only to death, following after our own passions and desires that ultimately produce pain instead of the pleasure they promise. Our sin means that we are entirely deserving of death, and in God's justice and goodness, He destroys evil with His wrath. God could send His wrath upon us all, but He chooses to make a way for mercy. As Romans 6:23 proclaims, "the wages of sin is death, but the gift of God is eternal life in Christ Jesus our Lord."

The gift of life is only possible through death. The Son of God became a human like us in order to save us. Jesus Christ was like us in every sense except for our sin. He lived a perfect life, fulfilling the covenant of works in our place, and then died a sinner's death. He became our new covenant head under a covenant of grace, in which we gain His righteousness as our own by grace alone through faith in Him. He took our sin upon Himself, becoming sin for us and then defeating it by dying on the cross. Three days later, He rose again from the grave, and all who have faith in Him are united to Him in His life. He earned the blessing of the covenant and gave it to us. He is working in us day by day to restore the image of God in us, and we will be totally sinless in His presence when He returns.

> The first gospel in Genesis 3:15 points to Jesus. He is the promised offspring of Eve whose heel would be bruised by the serpent.

The first gospel in Genesis 3:15 points to Jesus. He is the promised offspring of Eve whose heel would be bruised by the serpent. The serpent would wound, but he would not have victory over Christ. The suffering servant would endure the pain of the cross, but even His death would not be final. When Christ died on the cross, it seemed as if the devil had won and all hope was lost, but even though Satan bruised the Savior's heel, the wounds left by the serpent would be the very thing that would crush him under the feet of Jesus. Christ is not defeated in His death but is victorious over the power of sin and death in His resurrection.

The rest of the Bible tells the story of God bringing this promise of good news to pass. He is not a different God in the Old Testament than He is the New Testament; He works throughout all time to bring about redemption. He has been merciful and gracious from the beginning, planning to give the life of His Son for us before He ever created us. Throughout the rest of Genesis and the rest of the Old Testament, God's people are looking for, hoping for, and longing for the seed of the woman, the promised offspring who would crush the serpent's head and save God's people from their sins. We should read all of Scripture through the lens of this promise, and we should live all of our lives in light of the gospel. There is no page of God's Word and no area of life that is untouched by the gospel. May we take hold of it today and every day.

I will put hostility between you and the woman, and between your offspring and her offspring. He will strike your head, and you will strike his heel.

—

Genesis 3:15

TODAY'S QUESTIONS

In your own words, what is the gospel?

The gospel is the good news, Jesus coming back to those who have claimed him

What does the fact that God gave the gospel in the garden of Eden reveal about His character?

That he loved us before he knew us. That he is a gracious God

How does seeing that God promised Jesus in the beginning of Scripture change the way you read the rest of the Bible?

It gives an understanding of why God does what he does.

His
Blood
Cries
Out

His Blood Cries Out

"No act of injustice escapes God's sight."

In the midst of sorrow, God promised salvation. Adam and Eve would look for the promised offspring, and the beginning of Genesis 4 swells with the hope that the One who would right their wrongs had arrived. In faith, Eve joyfully proclaimed that she had given birth to another *ish,* another man, with the Lord's help. Eve believed the promise that God made in Genesis 3:15. Perhaps this child would be the promised One.

Eve gave birth to a second son named Abel. Scripture recounts a time when both sons made an offering to the Lord. The word "offering" refers to an offering of allegiance to God. God did not look favorably on Cain's offering of produce, but Abel's offering of the first and best of his flock was accepted. The primary cause for God's rejection of Cain's offering was not the content of the offering itself but his heart. While Cain claimed allegiance to God, his life did not reflect a heart that was committed to the Lord. Hebrews 11:4 reveals that Abel's offering was made in faith, but Cain's was not. Cain did not have faith in the Lord that would yield righteousness, but his hard heart produced arrogance and hatred. Cain's response reveals this arrogance; rather than recognizing his fault and humbling himself before the Lord, he became furious. The anger within him burned so intensely that it could not be hidden and was instead revealed by his contorted and downturned face.

The Lord graciously approached Cain to question him, much like He sought to draw out Adam's sin in the garden. God offered Cain a chance to repent and be restored. "If you do what is right, won't you be accepted?" The word "accepted" literally means uplifted. Cain's own sin was the reason for his downturned face, but God graciously offered to lift his countenance. God warned Cain what would happen if he continued in his sin instead of turning from it. God likened sin to a ravenous beast, crouched and ready to pounce on Cain to devour him. In grace, God urged Cain to turn from his wicked ways.

Cain ignored the words of the Lord and fell prey to his own sin. He brought Abel to a field and murdered him. Much like the account of Adam and Eve's choice to eat the forbidden fruit, the description is eerily simple, but the crime is devastating. In an act of hatred toward God, Cain destroyed his own brother. He was the first to take a fellow image bearer's life, following the example of the devil who was "a murderer from the beginning," leading deceived Eve to her death sentence (John 8:44).

As in Genesis 3, God immediately confronted Cain in his sin. God's words, "Where is your brother Abel?" mirror the "Where are you?" to Adam in Genesis 3:9. Cain's response was a deliberate lie, wrought with disdain and arrogance. One might imagine Cain with arms crossed, bitterly saying, "How should I know?" With Abel's body buried beneath the ground, Cain thought he could conceal his sin, but no sin evades the eye of the Lord. God's response, "What have you done?" emphasizes the pure evil of Cain's horrific act. God declared that the blood of Abel cried out to Him from the ground. No act of injustice escapes God's sight. He hears the cries of the oppressed. God's wrath punishes every wrong. Vengeance is His, and He will bring justice (Deuteronomy 32:35).

God pronounced a curse upon Cain. The ground that he spent his life working would no longer yield crops for him, and he would wander homeless on the earth away from God's presence. Cain cried out to the Lord, not in humble remorse, but to object to the severity of God's punishment. He feared for his life, likely assuming that someone would avenge the life of Abel by taking Cain's. God placed a mark upon Cain that would deter others from killing him. The curse still remained, but God's mercy extended as far as it could for an unrepentant heart. Just as Adam and Eve were sent out of God's presence, Cain also departed from the presence of the Lord and settled east of Eden in a land called Nod, which means wandering.

> The curse still remained, but God's mercy extended as far as it could for an unrepentant heart.

The parallels between Adam and Eve in the garden of Eden and the story of Cain in Genesis 4 reveal that sin was growing. The sinful nature that Adam and Eve unleashed in the garden could not be tamed. Just one generation later, the insidious effects of sin were painfully evident. Eve sinned when she was deceived, but now Cain rebelled even when God clearly warned him of his error. The curse affected not only the marriage relationship, but now brother rose up to kill brother. Adam and Eve rationalized their sin to God, but Cain answered with a blatant lie. Adam and Eve were humbled by their shame, but Cain responded in pride. Adam and Eve wanted to be like God, but Cain's hatred led him to kill one of God's image bearers. Eve had hoped Cain was the promised offspring, but his sin proved he was far from being sufficient to save. God's people would have to wait for His promise, but He would be faithful to fulfill it.

The blood of Abel the shepherd cried out for vengeance, but the blood of another shepherd speaks better things (Hebrews 12:24). The blood of Jesus Christ cries out for mercy and forgiveness. He is the true offspring. He fulfills the cries for vengeance by bearing God's wrath in our place. Because of His love for us, His perfect life, and His work on the cross, His blood means our righteousness. What glorious grace!

God's warning to Cain is a warning to all of us. Sin is not something to be taken lightly. It is not enough to say that we will not seek out sin, because it will seek us out. The description of the devil in 1 Peter 5:8 as a lion who prowls around seeking to devour someone bears a striking resemblance to God's description of sin in this passage. And so we must be on our guard. We must be alert. We must rule over our sin so that it does not rule over us. But we cannot rule over it on our own. We need the power of the Spirit of Christ to resist the devil and sin. If we will humble ourselves, confess our sin, and come to Christ as the only one who can make us righteous, by faith we can grow in Christlikeness and flee from sin.

and to Jesus, the mediator of a new covenant, and to the sprinkled blood, which says better things than the blood of Abel.

Hebrews 12:24

TODAY'S QUESTIONS

What similarities and differences do you see between Cain and his parents?
What do they reveal about sin after the garden?

-they sinned, didn't turn back to God.
Cain tried to hide Abel's death
Adam+Eve hid in the Garden

What does God's interaction with Cain reveal about God's character?

He is a forgiving God, He wants us
to turn away from our sin

What is your attitude toward your own sin? Is it something you think about?

I feel guilty after u have done something,
I replay it through out my mind, so
I think about it.

Waiting for the Off-spring

Waiting for the Offspring

"The cancer of sin was multiplying rapidly, and the longing for the promised offspring grew deeper."

Eve had hoped that her son, Cain, would be the promised offspring who would crush the head of the serpent, but his wickedness proved otherwise. The murder of Abel stood as evidence that sin was growing among mankind, and that pattern would continue in the coming generations.

Cain went on to have a son named Enoch, a name similar to the Hebrew word for initiate. He built a city, which can refer to even a very small group of people, and named it after his son. In the wake of God's curse that Cain would be a wanderer on the earth, it seems as if Cain defiantly tried to create for himself a new beginning. He would try to prove that he did not need God. From his family line came many technical advancements like music and metalworking, but his line would also proceed in great sin. Cain's descendant, Lamech, displayed tragic moral failure in taking two wives, a clear violation of God's design for marriage that He set forth in Eden. Lamech's polygamous marriage, however, was not the extent of his sinfulness.

The song of Lamech in verses 23 and 24 is a horrific picture of the utter wickedness of man after the fall. Not only did Lamech sin, but he reveled in it. In arrogance he called his two wives to hear his song as he boasted of murder. The Hebrew word used to describe the person he killed is *yeled*, which means child. When a mere child wounded Lamech, he took his life and rejoiced in his death. Cain tried to hide his murderous act, but Lamech wore it like a badge. The cancer of sin was multiplying rapidly, and the longing for the promised offspring grew deeper.

Even so, God had not abandoned His promise. God gave Adam and Eve another offspring named Seth. His name means appointed, and Eve held onto hope that God would not fail to appoint one of her offspring to be the Promised One. Seth was not the one they were waiting for, but God would bring about the seed through his line. God gave Seth to Eve in her grief of the two sons she had lost—one to murder and the other to sin—and Seth's birth is a picture of the restoration that was to come. The last two verses of Genesis 4 point to the true hope for salvation. In a world filled with wickedness and violence and all manner of sin, God's people must call upon His name. They must put their faith in the true offspring.

Chapter 5 begins a new section of Genesis, recounting the generations of Adam. The genealogies in the book of Genesis are not dry lists of names to be skimmed over. The announcement of each new name is full of anticipation as the people of God wonder, "Could this be the one?" The possibility of the promised seed's arrival is cut short with the refrain, "Then he died," of each passing generation. They were still waiting for the offspring.

There was one man in the generations of Adam, though, who did not follow the normal pattern of death. Enoch never tasted death, but God took him. Through years and years of waiting and disappointment, Enoch's deathless life served as a marker of God's faithfulness to His promise. Enoch is a reminder that death will not have the final word. God is the one who has the power to save, and all those who live according to God's commands by faith in the promised offspring, Jesus Christ—as Enoch walked with God by faith in the One to come—will not taste final death. Even if we experience physical death, those who put their hope in Jesus Christ will have life eternal.

> God is the one who has the power to save, and all those who live according to God's commands by faith in the promised offspring, Jesus Christ will not taste final death.

Genesis 5 ends with the birth of a son to Lamech. This is not the wicked Lamech from Cain's line, but he is a descendant of Seth like the others listed in chapter 5. Lamech names his son Noah. He believes that Noah will bring them "relief from the agonizing labor of [their] hands, caused by the ground the Lord has cursed." When God pronounced the curse of sin in Genesis 3, He said that the ground would be cursed, making work toilsome and difficult. Now Lamech hopes that Noah will bring them relief from their difficult labor. He hopes that Noah will be the offspring for whom they have so long awaited.

As we read about the growing wickedness after the fall, it ought to stir in our hearts a longing for the true offspring. Each new son who was born was insufficient to save a people cursed by sin, but the true Son of God is able to restore what sin destroyed. Jesus Christ is the one who was without sin in a depraved world. He is the only one with the power to defeat the devil. Only Christ could overcome death.

There are many times in our own lives that we must wait. Our seasons of waiting can leave us feeling weary and discouraged, but in the waiting, God is faithful. We can look back to the countless years that God's people waited for the Savior. When all hope seemed lost, God sent Jesus, the offspring of the woman, in the fullness of time (Galatians 4:4). We can remember that God's timing is not our own, and His timing is perfect. When it seems as if God has abandoned us, He is working still. As we wrestle with unmet desires, may our gaze be directed to Christ who fulfills every longing.

When it seems as if
God has abandoned us,
He is working still.

TODAY'S QUESTIONS

What does God's faithfulness to His promise to send a savior reveal about the way He relates to us?

That he is there working for us during our season of waiting.

Do you see boasting about sin in the world today? Do you see this tendency in your own life?

Boasting is evident about sin in the world. Many are glad about their sin.

Have you ever experienced a season of waiting? How can what you have read so far in Genesis encourage you as you wait?

The reading can encourage me because it reminds me that God is still working for me, even when I can't see or feel him. I have to trust that!

The Spread of Sin

The Spread of Sin

"Sin was growing worse, and the promise of the righteous offspring seemed further away than ever."

Sin was spreading like an infectious disease, contaminating every corner of creation. As chapter 6 opens, the increasing severity of sin is evident. The verses making up Genesis 6:1-4 are perhaps the mostly widely debated verses in the book of Genesis. Whichever way we interpret them, their significance is clear—the world was filled with wickedness. Some scholars argue that the daughters of men were the descendants of Cain and that the sons of God were the descendants of Seth. In this interpretation, the marriages of the Sethites to the ungodly Cainites resulted in the corruption of Seth's descendants. Other scholars argue that the sons of God, a term referring to angels in the Old Testament, were fallen angels. Desiring sexual relations, these demonic spirits left their proper place and inhabited human bodies to satisfy their urges. Both interpretations carry the same force—that unrestrained lust produced sexual perversion. Just as Eve saw the desirable fruit and took it, the sons of God saw that the daughters of man were attractive, and they took them as their own. Sin was growing worse, and the promise of the righteous offspring seemed further away than ever.

In response to the growing wickedness of man, God resolved to cut their lives short. His Spirit is what gave them life—the breath of God in their lungs—but God would remove it from them after 120 years. This period of time could indicate the length of time between God's declaration of judgment and the coming of the flood, or it could refer to the gradual shortening of the human life span that is evidenced later in Genesis. The text talks about the Nephilim, the offspring of the marriages between the sons of God and the daughters of man. Nephilim literally means fallen ones, and their name matches their corrupt nature. They were mighty men, violent warriors, and sexual aggressors who were held in high esteem by the world. New birth would have been entirely beautiful under God's command to be fruitful and multiply, but sin perverted God's good creation, and multiplication meant more evil instead of good.

The declaration, "The Lord saw," at the beginning of verse 5 is a lamentable reversal of God looking upon His finished work of creation in Genesis 1:31. Once He saw His creation and declared it very good, but in the days of Noah, the Lord looked upon His creation and saw only wickedness. The strong language of verse 5 leaves no room for question. Every one of man's thoughts, every one of his motivations, and every one of his actions was only evil all the time. There was no glimpse of goodness. There was no momentary flicker of virtue. Humanity was totally and utterly depraved.

God's response to the wickedness that had infested His good creation was unimaginable sorrow and burning anger. His beautiful and pure creation was utterly desecrated, and He was deeply grieved. The text says that God regretted that He had made man. This statement does not mean that God made a mistake or that He was somehow surprised by sin. On the contrary, God created the world and humanity with the full knowledge that to save them would come at a great cost to Himself. Rather, this language expresses God's intense hatred for sin. It speaks of His deep sadness over His beautiful world and over the image bearers now bearing the mark of sin. Sin grieves God to His core because it runs contrary to everything that He is—the holy, pure, and glorious God of creation.

> In exercising judgment and wiping out the sin-infected world, God in his grace protects His creation from the destructiveness of sin.

God resolved to bring judgment upon mankind for their sinful ways. Sin always merits the judgment of God, and the intensity and scope of God's judgment here illuminate the pervasiveness and severity of sin. The flood would blot out all of humanity and destroy all life on earth as every corner of creation was infected by sin. In exercising judgment and wiping out the sin-infected world, God in his grace protects His creation from the destructiveness of sin. Wickedness would not prevail.

The people of God had been waiting for the promised offspring, and the waning hope that a righteous seed could come from such a wicked world seems to be completely extinguished with God's decision to obliterate humanity. Yet, even in the midst of great sin and great judgment, God did not forget His promise. God would enact His righteous judgment on a world tainted by sin. Even still, God showed grace. God would preserve a small part of the human race along with His promise of the offspring. Genesis 6:8 reveals that Noah found favor with God. The word "favor" is more often translated as grace. This favor was not based on any goodness that Noah possessed but was purely on God's unmerited grace. In fact, Hebrews 11:7 confirms that Noah's righteousness came not by being sinless but by faith. God's favor toward Noah is hope, not just for Him but for all who put their faith in the offspring.

Sin is detestable. It is not something to boast in but something to mourn over. All sin is rightly subject to God's vengeance, and He enacts justice by punishing sin. In Matthew 24, Jesus says that God's judgment in the days of Noah points forward to another judgment when Christ returns again and judges the world. No sin will go unpunished, but all will be made right at the second coming of Jesus. We must acknowledge the reality that judgment is coming. Apart from the grace of God, Christ's return is a terrifying thing, and we must not go on living under the assumption that we will face no repercussions. However, if we believe the gospel and put our hope in Christ, we do not have to fear the judgment. Christ has taken our punishment upon Himself, and He has given us His righteousness.

God meets sin with wrathful judgment and unfathomable grace. These realities are not contradictory but are perfectly displayed at the cross. There is no sin that will go unpunished and no wrong that will not be righted. Every one of us will either receive the judgment for our own sin, or that judgment will be laid on Christ in our place. May we run to Him as the giver of grace.

Sin grieves God to His core because it runs contrary to everything that He is—the holy, pure, and glorious God of creation.

TODAY'S QUESTIONS

This passage gives a disturbing picture of the evil that sin produces. How should this knowledge impact your attitude toward the sin in your own life?

It makes me want to stay away from sin, and have no part of it.

What is God's response to sin? What does this reveal about His character?

It grieved him, and he destroyed sin.

That he is a just God, but also a caring and loving God because he found favor w/ Noah

How does the depth of human sin described in this passage impact your understanding of God's grace?

It shows that

Noah Walked *with* God

Noah Walked with God

"He will not forget His covenant of grace."

In response to the anticipation created by verse 8 with its statement that Noah found favor with God, verse 9 begins a new section with another *toledot*. This section continues all the way through the end of chapter 9. The story of Noah has a very intentional literary structure. It forms a chiasm, meaning the ideas expressed in the first half of the section are paralleled in reverse order in the second half, forming an x-shaped structure (see outline on page 111). The first half of the chiasm is a sort of decreation, an undoing of what God has made in Genesis 1. The turning point of the chiasm is, "God remembered Noah," in Genesis 8:1. The second half of the section mirrors the first in reverse order with recreation. The structure of this section emphasizes that though God brings judgment, He intends to save a people for Himself through a deliverer. It points to God's faithfulness to His promises to bring about the promised offspring. He will not forget His covenant of grace. It illustrates God's commitment to restore His good creation that was perverted by sin.

All of mankind has been described as wholly wicked, but this passage says that Noah was righteous. While the world around him gloated in their sin, indulging in violence and sexual immorality, Noah was the only one who was blameless. This is not to say that Noah was without sin, as subsequent chapters will clearly illustrate, but that his life was marked by obedience to God that proceeds from faith. Noah could not be described as righteous because of his own good deeds but because God showed him favor. Through faith in the promised offspring to come, Noah received God's abundant and transforming grace. While his contemporaries lived in corruption, Noah preached righteousness (2 Peter 2:5). Like the once sinless Adam in the garden, or Enoch who did not taste death, Noah walked with God. Throughout the story of Noah, Moses will show how he was a second Adam, God's representative in the new creation after the flood. Even the statement in verse 10 that Noah had three sons mirrors Adam's three sons.

Verses 10 and 11 reiterate the depravity of the world. God had formed the earth and filled it with good things, but now it was filled with wickedness. The word "corrupt" is repeated in different forms three times in these two verses and describes the destruction that would come as a result of the wickedness now in the world. Although God would destroy them with the flood, these verses illustrate that they brought destruction upon themselves. Their sin was the reason for God's judgment, because "every creature had corrupted its way." God told Noah of His divine plan: to destroy the already corrupted earth.

In light of the impending judgment, God told Noah to build an ark. He intended to destroy the earth and its inhabitants, but He also meant to save Noah and his family. The ark would be the vehicle through which Noah would pass through the waters of judgment and live.

The ark would be gigantic, spanning 450 feet—the length of one and a half football fields. It would take decades to build. All the while, the sinful world looked on, likely mocking and ridiculing Noah as he and his sons chopped down tree after tree, drove in spike after spike, and covered the monstrosity of an ark with pitch. God commanded Noah to give it three levels with eighteen inches between the tops of the walls and the roof where light and fresh air could enter. The work of building the ark would have been an all-consuming endeavor.

> God would destroy every living creature, but He would not abandon His promises or His plan for a beautiful creation.

After God gave the initial instructions for building the ark, He revealed the method of destruction—He would destroy the world with a flood, undoing what He made in creation. Where once God separated the waters from the waters with land, He would now pummel the waters upon the earth in destruction. God would destroy every living creature, but He would not abandon His promises or His plan for a beautiful creation. The massive size of the ark was meant to accommodate animals. God told Noah to bring in a male and female of every kind of animal as well as every kind of food. Through these animals and Noah's family, God would once again populate and fill the earth.

God guaranteed the salvation of Noah and the renewal of the earth by promising to establish His covenant with Noah. After Adam and Eve sinned, He enacted a covenant of grace so that all who place their hope in the promised offspring would be saved by God's grace through faith in Him. Even though God planned to destroy the earth and all of its inhabitants, He intended to establish His covenant with Noah, carrying on the covenant of grace through him. Through Noah's line, the promise of the offspring would still stand.

The chapter closes with a statement of Noah's response; Noah did what God commanded him to do. The repetition in verse 22 emphasizes Noah's obedience. He was a man who walked with God in obedience to His commands. This man is a picture of those whom God saves. However, we must be careful not to think that God saved Noah because He was obedient. Noah was righteous, Noah walked in obedience, and Noah was blameless because of God's grace to him. Faith in God produces obedience. Faith produces good works. Noah could never earn God's grace, and neither can we. When we stop trusting in our own works to save us and trust instead in the work of Christ, we are transformed. The evidence of faith in God is obedience to His commands.

And Noah did this. He did everything that God had commanded him.

—

Genesis 6:22

A. Noah Introduced (6:9)

B. Noah's Sons (6:10)

C. Corruption and Violence (6:11-12)

D. God will destroy the earth (6:13)

E. God commands Noah to build the ark (6:14-22)

F. God commands Noah to go into the ark (7:1-3)

G. Waiting seven days for the flood (7:4-10)

H. The flood begins (7:11-15)

I. God closes the door (7:16)

J. 40 days of flood (7:17-18)

K. Water covers the mountains (7:19-20)

L. Waters remain for 150 days (7:21-24)

M. GOD REMEMBERS NOAH (8:1)

L. Waters recede for 150 days (8:1-5)

K. Mountains are visible (8:5)

J. 40 days of flood come to an end (8:6)

I. Noah opens a window (8:6)

H. Raven and Dove leave (8:7-9)

G. Waiting seven days for the waters to recede (8:10-14)

F. God commands Noah to exit the ark (8:15-19)

E. Noah builds an altar (8:20)

D. God will preserve the earth (8:21-22)

C. Blessing of the covenant (9:1-17)

B. Noah's Sons (9:18-27)

A. Noah's death (9:28-29)

TODAY'S QUESTIONS

Based on the story of Genesis up to this point, what do you think God's purpose was in sparing Noah and his family?

He knew Noah would be obedient and follow his commands

Numerous decades would pass between the time that God commanded Noah to build the ark and the beginning of the flood. What does Noah's obedience reveal about what he believed to be true about God?

Noah obeyed God based on the promise of a future. How should God's future promises impact the way you live now?

The same as Noah's. God has promised us eternal life if we accept him and be obedient.

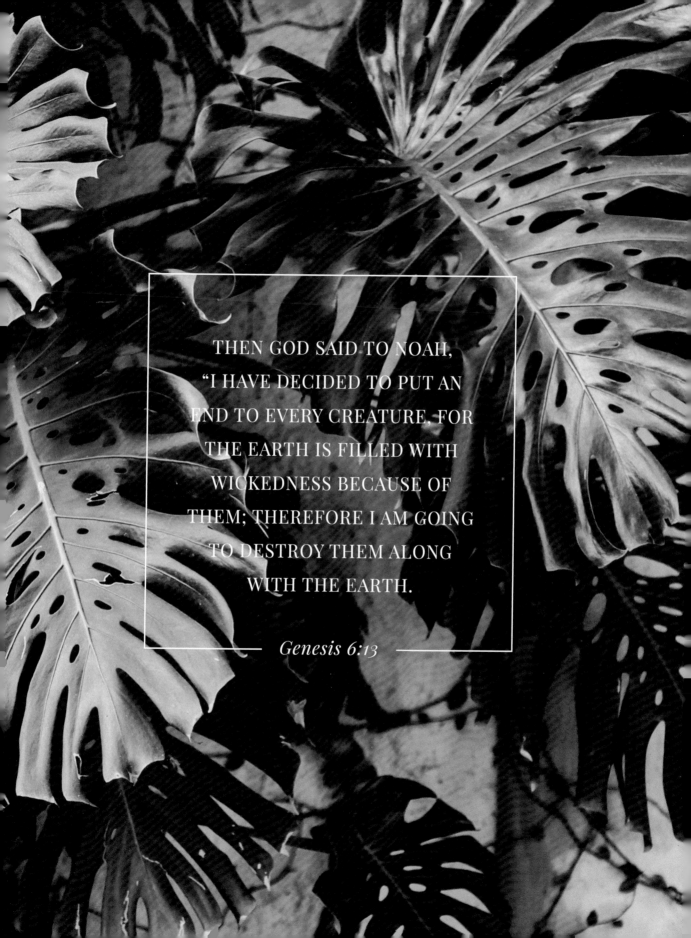

THEN GOD SAID TO NOAH,
"I HAVE DECIDED TO PUT AN
END TO EVERY CREATURE, FOR
THE EARTH IS FILLED WITH
WICKEDNESS BECAUSE OF
THEM; THEREFORE I AM GOING
TO DESTROY THEM ALONG
WITH THE EARTH.

Genesis 6:13

IF YOU DO WHAT IS RIGHT, WON'T YOU BE ACCEPTED? BUT IF YOU DO NOT DO WHAT IS RIGHT, SIN IS CROUCHING AT THE DOOR. ITS DESIRE IS FOR YOU, BUT YOU MUST RULE OVER IT.

Genesis 4:7

Paraphrase the passage from this week.

_____
_____
_____
_____
_____
_____
_____
_____
_____
_____
_____
_____
_____

What did you observe from this week's text about God and His character?

_____
_____
_____
_____
_____
_____
_____
_____

What does this week's passage reveal about the condition of mankind and about yourself?

_____

_____

_____

_____

How does this passage point to the gospel?

_____

_____

_____

_____

_____

How should you respond to this passage? What is the personal application?

_____

_____

_____

_____

What specific action steps can you take this week to apply this passage?

_____

_____

_____

_____

_____

Sealed
and
Safe

Sealed and Safe

"Like Abraham who would come after him, Noah's faith in God was counted to him as righteousness, but as with us, sin remained until Christ's second coming."

God warned Noah of the coming flood and gave him instructions for building the ark. In the beginning of chapter 7, God gave Noah additional instructions about bringing the animals into the ark and entering it with his family, as well as further information about the duration and effects of the flood. The remainder of the chapter recounts the events that occurred just as God said they would. He would certainly be true to His word.

The time was drawing near for the promised flood waters to come. God commanded Noah to enter the ark with his wife and his three sons along with their wives and to bring into the ark every kind of animal. The command to bring seven pairs of some animals is not in contrast to God's previous command to bring two of each kind. The general command was one pair, while the sets of seven animals are the exception. The inclusion of these extra animals was necessary for sacrifice, and it anticipates Noah's sacrifice after the flood as well as the establishment of the sacrificial system given to Moses. These animals serve as a reminder that although God was bringing judgment on sin, it was not the final judgment. The forgiveness of sin requires sacrifice, and as fallen humans, Noah and his family would bring sin into the post flood world. Like Abraham who would come after him, Noah's faith in God was counted to him as righteousness (Genesis 15:6), but as with us, sin remained until Christ's second coming.

God gave Noah a seven-day time period between the command to enter the ark and the start of the flood, during which time Noah brought in the animals. God's undoing of creation was looming, and just as God created the earth in seven days, He warned Noah seven days before He destroyed it. At the end of this time period, He would blot out every living creature, completely wiping them from the face of the earth.

The description of Noah in 6:22 is repeated in 7:5, as well as later in 7:9 and 7:16—Noah did what the Lord commanded him to do. He was a man whose life was marked by an obedience that stems from faith. He entered the ark with his family and every kind of animal just as God had commanded. When they were all safely inside, God shut him in. His divine seal would mean that though every living thing on the ground would be destroyed, Noah could not be touched.

And then the waters came. The language of this passage indicates that what came upon the earth was no mere rainstorm. The great deluge formed as the water burst forth from above and below, violently rising, surging, raging, and bringing utter destruction. The torrential rains pelted the ground from the sky, and great fountains erupted from the ground below. Gone was the orderly separation of the waters above and below from Genesis 1. The earth God formed was destroyed beneath a tumultuous, watery mass. The water rose so high that the mountain tops were completely submerged. Nothing on the ground survived. How great is God's wrath against wickedness, and how revolting the sin in which mankind delights!

God's judgment did not come without warning. 2 Peter 2:5 reveals that Noah had preached righteousness and that God had waited patiently to send the flood to allow for repentance. Still, the world walked in disobedience, chasing after sinful passions, while Noah alone walked with God. Even now, the Lord waits to bring the greater judgment so that all who will come to Him will repent, but judgment is coming. May we turn away from sin and walk with God by grace through faith in Jesus Christ.

> Even now, the Lord waits to bring the greater judgment so that all who will come to Him will repent, but judgment is coming.

God's salvation of Noah and his family is a picture of the greater deliverance that Christ would accomplish on the cross. Noah was hidden in the ark with the door sealed by God and protected from judgment, but his true hope, and ours, is in a greater ark. By faith in Jesus, we are "hidden with Christ in God" (Colossians 3:3). He is our protection from judgment. Through Christ, we who believe are held securely in the Father's hand, and no one can ever snatch us out (John 10:28). In Christ, though we stand before God on that final judgment day, we will not be touched by God's wrath because Christ has taken it for us. We are covered by His blood and given His righteousness.

TODAY'S QUESTIONS

Imagine being in Noah's position during the days before the flood and then when the waters came. What kinds of emotions do you think he may have experienced?

Concerned, that he may not have enough time honored that God chose him to build the arc

What does God sealing the door to the ark reveal about our own salvation?

That once we are saved, He has sealed our hearts and we are written down in the lambs book of life

How can Noah's journey on the ark encourage you in your own times of turmoil?

He was obedient to God even he wasn't sure.

It reminds us that we need to be obedient even when we are going through things and God will help us out.

God Remembered

God Remembered

"When God remembers something in Scripture, it does not imply that He forgot. Rather, God's remembering is associated with divine action."

God was destroying the earth with the flood waters, but Genesis 8:1 marks a turning point. It is the center of the chiasm of Noah's life, marking the moment when decreation turns to recreation. God had sent the flood, and Noah and his family were tucked away inside the ark. The gigantic ark seemed much smaller among the crashing waves and raging waters. All life was being destroyed around them, while Noah and his family were sealed inside the ark in the dark, thrown about on the water, the sound of rain pounding against the walls of the ark. According to all human reason, they too would perish in the flood, but God remembered Noah. This fact was the difference between life and death. When God remembers something in Scripture, it does not imply that He forgot. Rather, God's remembering is associated with divine action. For God to remember Noah meant that He remembered the promise He made to him, and He would move to bring it to pass. God would be faithful to His covenant.

God acted by causing a wind to blow over the face of the earth. The Hebrew word *ruach* means wind and spirit. The wind blowing over the waters recalls the Spirit hovering over the waters in Genesis 1:2. Creation had been destroyed, but God was beginning afresh. The process of recreation was commencing. The same God who released the raging waters upon the earth now caused the rain to stop and the fountains to close. Slowly the waters began to dry up, and the ark came to rest atop a mountain somewhere in modern day Turkey.

After forty days and nights of rain, plus another 150 days until the ark rested on the mountaintop, the wait was not yet over for Noah and his family. We can imagine the possible range of emotions for the people aboard the ship. Perhaps they feared for their lives as they wondered if God would indeed save them. Maybe at times the boredom and monotony of day after day inside the ark, feeding and tending to the animals seemed too much to bear. Bickering and frustration likely occurred as in-laws lived under one roof in a time of great stress. Surely they longed to get off the boat, but still they had to wait. The water slowly continued to dry up, revealing the remaining mountaintops. After more than eight months closed into the ark, Noah sent out a raven, a bird that would fly toward land and was used to see which direction land could be found. The bird did not return, so apparently land was beginning to appear. He then sent out a dove three times. Doves have a shorter flying range and were often sent out of ships to see if land was nearby. The first time, there was nowhere for it to land because the waters had not sufficiently receded. The second time, it brought back a fresh olive branch — evidence that not only were the waters going down but that God was indeed bringing forth new life on the earth He had destroyed. The olive branch was a beacon of hope and a signal of restoration. The third time the dove did not return, indicating that the waters had completely receded, and the dove had found a place to rest. The waiting was long, but Noah waited patiently for the Lord. In due time, after 371 days on the ark, the ground was dry.

> God had given a new beginning — a fresh start. But even this second beginning would not be the last.

At long last, God commanded Noah and his family to go out of the ark and bring the animals with them. The animals were to be fruitful and multiply — a phrase that hearkens back to the creation mandate God gave to Adam and Eve. The empty land that had been decimated would be filled once again as the animals swarmed on the earth.

God had given a new beginning—a fresh start. But even this second beginning would not be the last. This judgment and subsequent recreation were antecedents of the final judgment and subsequent new heaven and new earth. The account of the flood is both a somber warning and a sweet comfort. It is a call for sinners to repent and turn to Jesus, the true ark who can carry us safely through judgment. It is also a call for those who are in Christ to take heart. The world still bears the marks of the curse. We are surrounded by wickedness and sin, but it will not always be this way. Christ will come again in judgment, ridding the world of all evil, even down to the sin remaining in our hearts. We will be wholly pure. We will dwell forever in the new heaven and new earth without the sting of death, the corruption of sin, or the shame of disobedience. The waiting may feel long, but the Lord will be faithful. On that day, we will truly and fully walk with God.

God is a God who remembers His promises. He is always faithful to His covenants. If we have put our faith in Christ, we are saved under the covenant of grace, and we can be confident that God will bring us safely home to Him. Whether we endure suffering that bears upon us like waves slamming against the ark or long seasons of waiting like Noah and His family waiting for the waters to recede, we can be confident that God will be faithful to us.

God is a God who remembered
His promises. He is always faithful
to His covenants.

126

TODAY'S QUESTIONS

What change do you notice in the text after the statement that God remembered Noah in 8:1?

That things began to slow down, and the waters started to recede.

Read back through the text. Use the space below to note each reference to a length of time that Noah and his family had to wait for the flood to stop and the waters to recede.

150 days. 40 days, 7 days, 7 days

When is a time when you have experienced a season of waiting? What does Noah's long stay on the ark reveal about God's character in our waiting?

That he is there in our season and have not forgotten us. We just need to be obedient.

Grace *and* Sacrifice

Grace and Sacrifice

"By grace, God delivered Noah and his family safely through the waters of judgment to the new creation."

By grace, God delivered Noah and his family safely through the waters of judgment to the new creation. When Noah exited the ark, he set up an altar and made sacrifices. He took clean animals and offered them as burnt offerings to God. In the law, God made a distinction between clean animals that could be offered for sacrifice and unclean animals. Although God had not given the law in its entirety at this point, He revealed elements of the law, such as sacrificial laws, to Noah. Noah's immediate response to God's grace to Him is worship. Noah's worshipful sacrifice was a sacrifice of dedication. In giving the burnt offerings, Noah expressed that his life was wholly given to God. It was also an offering of propitiation, which means a sacrifice that puts someone in right standing with God where the relationship was broken by sin. The text says that the sacrifice was a pleasing aroma to God. Unlike the unacceptable offering of wicked Cain, God accepted the offering that Noah made in faith. The word "pleasing" has the sense of soothing. The Hebrew word is *nichowach* and is very similar to Noah's name, *Noach*. This play on words recalls Genesis 5:29 when Lamech gave Noah the name that means rest out of hope that God would bring them relief from the effects of the curse. God's anger was soothed by Noah's sacrifice, and in response, the Lord vowed not to curse the ground again. He was not revoking the curse that He pronounced on the ground in Genesis 3:17, as the word for curse is different in both instances, but rather, he was resolving never again to destroy the earth with a flood.

God did not make this promise because the world was rid of sin. On the contrary, He stated in verse 21 that He would never again curse the ground "even though the inclination of the human heart is evil from youth onward." God vowed to withhold the fullness of His wrath despite the sinfulness of the human heart. His promise was not based on human merit but on grace made possible through sacrifice.

The small sacrifice that Noah made was not enough to atone for His sins, much less the sins of humanity, but it points to the greater sacrifice. Jesus Christ is the once for all sacrifice, the perfect offering atoning for all the sins of God's people. He is the righteous one in 1 Peter 3 who suffered once for the sins of the unrighteous. It is because of this great sacrifice that we are able to experience mercy and grace, without which we would receive the wrath of God. The fullness of that wrath is laid upon Christ, and we, in turn, receive the blessings of the covenant, fulfilled in the righteousness of Christ. Just as Noah and his family were delivered through the floodwaters to safety, we too are delivered through sin and suffering to God.

> God has given us immeasurable grace, and so in response we will live all our lives in worship to Him.

Verse 22 closes the chapter with a comforting promise: God will preserve the earth until the final judgment. In poetic beauty, God expresses that He is not only the Creator but also the Sustainer. The sun will continue to rise and set as God commands it to do so. The seasons will change under His divine guidance. God will once again bring an end to the world's current state and renew His glorious creation, but until then, we can rest assured that the world will keep on turning.

As those saved by God through the work of Jesus Christ, we have received the once for all sacrifice of Jesus. There is no more need to offer animal sacrifices, and nothing we do or give can save us. But just as Noah responded to God's grace in worship, so too should we. In Paul's letter to the Romans, he speaks of another sacrifice, not in order to gain mercy but because we have received mercy. We are called to offer our bodies as living sacrifices as a spiritual act of worship. God has given us immeasurable grace, and so in response we will live all our lives in worship to Him. Our sacrifice will be acceptable when it is not done to earn God's favor but is in response to His favor. To offer our bodies as living sacrifices is to walk in obedience to God. Like Noah, by God's grace, we walk with Him.

TODAY'S QUESTIONS

How does the offering of Noah differ from the offering of Cain in Genesis 4?

God was pleased with it.
It was given from the heart

Read Hebrews 10:12–14. How does Noah's sacrifice point forward to the death of Christ?

He sacrificed His son and sat down
on the right hand of God

What does verse 22 reveal about God's character?

That God cares for his people. He
wants us to know that because of
him we have the seasons, day and
night.

Man Re-commis-sioned

Man Recommissioned

"God brought judgment on a wicked world, but Noah and his family would bring sin with them through the flood."

When God created Adam and Eve, He blessed them and commissioned them to be His viceroys, or co-rulers, on the earth. The first humans failed miserably, sinning against God and bringing the curse of sin upon all the earth. Today's passage recounts the re-commissioning of man, closely mirroring that of Adam and Eve. However, this new world was tainted by sin, and the effects of sin are evident in the deviations from God's original creation mandate.

God repeated the same blessing He gave to Adam and Eve in Genesis 1:28 — to be fruitful and multiply and fill the earth. The earth was empty once again, and Noah's family and the animals would be the ones to repopulate it once more. Like their first parents, Noah and his family would have dominion over the animals, but instead of an amicable relationship between man and animal, the animals would submit to humans out of fear. God also gave humanity the animals for food. Some scholars argue that this practice already existed, whether with or without God's permission, while others say it was instituted for the first time here. However, God's permission to eat animals was not without restriction. They were not to eat the animal with the lifeblood still in it. In Scripture, the blood of a living being represents its life, and all life belongs to God. This command also pointed forward to the sacrificial system, in which the blood of an animal is given to atone for, or cover, the sins of God's people.

God's concern for the lifeblood of animals turns to the lifeblood of humans. If God gave restrictions for the lifeblood of animals that humans are permitted to eat, how much greater concern would God show for the lifeblood of humans! God stated that anyone who takes the life of a human, whether it be an animal or a fellow human, must in turn have his own life taken. There is much debate among Christians about the application of this passage today. Some argue that these verses unequivocally support the use of capital punishment, while others argue that these verses do not support the death penalty in the modern day after Christ's first coming. Wherever we fall in this argument, we must acknowledge that the strong statement that God makes in these verses speaks volumes about the value of human life. God gives His reason for this kind of penalty for shedding the blood of a human in Genesis 9:6 stating, "for God made humans in his image." Human life is sacred and elevated far above animal life because humans are made after God's likeness.

God's declaration about murder is another poignant reminder that the flood did not bring an end to sin. God brought judgment on a wicked world, but Noah and his family would bring sin with them through the flood. There would be no need for discussion about murder if sin had been eradicated. On the other hand, God also confirmed that though sin had marred the image of God in humans, that image was not totally lost. All human life was and still is intrinsically valuable because every human life bears the image of God.

In light of God's elevation of human life and serious words against murder, God repeats His command to be fruitful and multiply, calling them to multiply greatly on the earth. While some would seek to take life, God told Noah and his family to multiply it, filling the earth with image bearers once again.

> Human life is sacred. In fact, God values life so highly that He gave His only Son to die so that lives might be saved.

Human life is sacred. In fact, God values life so highly that He gave His only Son to die so that lives might be saved. As God's representatives on earth, we are called to treat our fellow humans with the same love, dignity, and respect as Christ treats us. Too often we devalue human life with slanderous words, selfish attitudes, and harmful actions. To treat our fellow image bearers with hatred, indifference, or contempt is to misrepresent the heart of God and to sin against Him.

After judgment, God brought forth new life. The presence of sin still lingered, and the new creation that God brought forth leaves us longing for something even greater. God will judge and renew once again, but sin will be no more. The story of Noah calls us to look ever forward to that day.

TODAY'S QUESTIONS

Re-read Genesis 1:28-31. What similarities and differences do you see between today's passage and God's commissioning of Adam and Eve?

to be fruitful and multiply
eat of the living things

What does today's passage reveal about the value of human life?
How does it differ from animal life?

Human life is favorably and God values it
So highly

What are some ways that human life is devalued today?
What would viewing human life as sacred look like practically?

lives are taken, looked down upon, talked
about, become arrogant

-Not taking a life, being kind to each
and everyone

A Gracious Covenant

A Gracious Covenant

*"God is always faithful to His covenants.
He comes through on every promise."*

When God brought Noah out of the ark, He made a covenant with him. A covenant is an unbreakable agreement between two or more parties. Covenants frequently have terms that each party must uphold, and the adherence to those terms often brings consequences: blessings for obedience and curses for disobedience. Covenants are deeply personal. To enter into a covenant is to enter into a binding relationship with someone. God is always faithful to His covenants. He comes through on every promise. Although God made covenants with man previously in Scripture, the establishment of the Noahic covenant is the first time Scripture uses the word "covenant." It is clear from this covenant that God still intended to fulfill His original purpose for the world since the dawn of creation—a world filled with God's image bearers to reflect His glory in His created order. He promised to never again destroy the earth and cut off all life with the waters of the flood. God does not intend to forfeit his plan for the world because of human sin.

The covenant that God made with Noah was universal. It was not just between God and Noah but extended to all of humanity and all of the animals and beasts of the earth, showing God's intention to preserve not just His people but His creation and created order. Under the Noahic covenant, God's grace extends to all as He keeps the world spinning in orbit in the perfect place to support life, sends rain to bring forth food, and restrains sin to sustain His image bearers. This grace is called common grace because it is universally given to all people. Without God's common grace that He promised in the Noahic covenant, the order of the universe would turn to chaos. God is the one who holds all things together.

In addition to common grace, the Noahic covenant also makes a way for God's redeeming grace. While all experience common grace, redeeming grace is reserved for those who put their faith in Jesus Christ, the promised offspring of Genesis 3:15. Without God's promise to preserve humanity, Eve's family line would be cut off, and the hope of the offspring would be lost. God could have destroyed the world and everything in it, but He made a promise in the garden, and He is always faithful to His promises. God's covenant of grace would still come to pass. Noah was not the promised offspring, but he points forward to the greater offspring to come. Through Noah, God delivered eight people and the animals through the waters of judgment, but through Jesus Christ, God will deliver all of His people.

Unlike some other covenants, there were no terms that Noah had to uphold. Like the covenant of grace that God established in Genesis 3:15, God alone initiated the covenant, and it was completely dependent on Him. As the rest of Scripture shows, this is the way that God works. If His promises were dependent upon us, everyone would fail, but it is God's very nature to be faithful to His covenants. We can trust every one.

> Like the covenant of grace that God established in Genesis 3:15, God alone initiated the covenant, and it was completely dependent on Him.

As a sign and a seal of the covenant He made that day, God set a rainbow in the sky. The beauty and brilliance of the rainbow against the dark clouds of the storm are a picture of God's judgment and mercy. It is a reminder of God's faithfulness to keep His promise to sustain the earth to the end, but it is also a reminder of His mercy toward us in *the rainbow* withholding the wrath that our sins merit. In Scripture, the rainbow is associated with God's glory. Nowhere do we see the glory of God's judgment and mercy more perfectly displayed than in the cross of Christ. He took the wrath of God for us in order that we may receive mercy. God's judgment fell upon Him so that we might live. He is our assurance that God will be merciful and faithful to us despite our sin and the evil around us. As we see God's bow in the sky, may we remember God's faithfulness. May we look back to the flood, but may we ultimately look to Jesus.

TODAY'S QUESTIONS

Grace is God's undeserved favor to sinners. How does the covenant He makes in today's passage display God's grace?

It is displayed by the rainbow. He shows favors on his people. and the land.

How does the Noahic Covenant correspond with God's original promise to Adam and Eve to send an offspring who would defeat Satan?

The covenant he made with Noah is universal, that he extends His grace to everyone

What evidence do you see in the world today that God's covenant with Noah still stands?

We still see the rainbow in the sky after it rains or storms.

THE LORD IS
GOOD TO EVERYONE;
HIS COMPASSION RESTS
ON ALL HE HAS MADE.

Psalm 145:9

AS LONG AS THE EARTH ENDURES, SEEDTIME AND HARVEST, COLD AND HEAT, SUMMER AND WINTER, AND DAY AND NIGHT WILL NOT CEASE.

———————

Genesis 8:22

Paraphrase the passage from this week.

_____
_____
_____
_____
_____
_____
_____
_____
_____
_____
_____
_____
_____
_____

What did you observe from this week's text about God and His character?

_____
_____
_____
_____
_____
_____
_____
_____

What does this week's passage reveal about the condition of mankind and about yourself?

_____

_____

_____

_____

How does this passage point to the gospel?

_____

_____

_____

_____

How should you respond to this passage? What is the personal application?

_____

_____

_____

_____

What specific action steps can you take this week to apply this passage?

_____

_____

_____

_____

_____

Shame *Exposed,* Shame *Covered*

Shame Exposed, Shame Covered

*"Like all who are saved by grace, Noah still battled the fallen nature.
Noah still desperately needed God's mercy and grace."*

Immediately after Moses recounts the covenant that God made with Noah, he shifts focus to Noah's sons, Shem, Ham, and Japheth. The text states right from the beginning that Ham is the father of Canaan. For the original Israelite audience, this name would have had great significance. The Canaanites would become the enemies of Israel, a wicked people who lived according to their sinful passions. Juxtaposed against the glory of God's promise to Noah's family, the mention of Canaan signals that something is about to go terribly wrong.

The text turns again to Noah many years after the flood. Enough time had passed for his children to have children. Noah worked the ground, and he planted a vineyard. From the vineyard he made wine. One day, Noah started drinking, but instead of practicing wise constraint, he drank more than he should have. His drinking was so excessive that he became drunk and apparently so drunk that he did not know when people came into his tent. In his heavily inebriated state, Noah stripped himself of his clothes and lay naked in his tent. This man who was heralded as the only righteous and blameless man in all the world drank himself into a stupor in the privacy of his own home. His failure to practice self-control and godly wisdom left him naked and shameful. Noah's sin is a poignant reminder that his righteousness was never his own. The righteousness of God was credited to Noah on account of his faith. Like all who are saved by grace, Noah still battled the fallen nature. Noah still desperately needed God's mercy and grace.

In Scripture, nakedness after the fall of man is closely associated with shame. When Adam and Eve ate the forbidden fruit in the garden of Eden, they became filled with shame over their own nakedness. In this new world, Noah's shameful nakedness resulted from overindulging in the fruit of the vine. As a kind of second Adam, Noah fell into sin just like the first one did. This story leaves no question that sin made its way into the new world. Noah and his family were impacted by original sin just like the rest of mankind, but because God promised to bring about an offspring through Eve, He spared her descendant. He spared sinful Noah.

It is at this point that Ham, the father of Canaan, enters the story. Ham came into his father's tent and found Noah unconscious and exposed. Rather than seeking to cover his father's shame, he exposed it even further. He left Noah uncovered in his tent and went out to tell his brothers what he had seen. Ham's actions indicate a sense of delighting in the downfall of another. In a blatant violation of the fifth commandment to honor father and mother, Ham found great satisfaction in telling his brothers about his father's disgraceful state.

Ham's gossip did not gain the reception he had likely hoped for from his brothers. They did not sneer and joke about Noah's nakedness, but they covered it. With a garment of clothing over their shoulders, Shem and Japheth walked backwards into Noah's tent and covered him. They did not chuckle between themselves as they sneaked a peak at their elderly father sprawled out on the ground. Rather, they took great pains to ensure that they did not look at him. Their hearts were sincere, and in that moment, they reflected the heart of God. The God who covered the nakedness of Adam and Eve with animal skins is the same God who covers our shame with the blood of Christ. Shem and Japheth covered their father with a garment of cloth, but Jesus clothes us with garments of salvation and robes of righteousness (Isaiah 61:10).

> Jesus is the true and better Noah who lived as a human with all of the temptations and difficulties of life in a fallen world yet never sinned.

The sins of Noah and Ham are evidence that though God had brought judgment through the flood, He did not fully eradicate sin. Noah was not the offspring who would crush the head of the serpent and defeat sin, but he pointed to the One who would. Jesus is the true and better Noah who lived as a human with all of the temptations and difficulties of life in a fallen world yet never sinned. He is the true and better deliverer who would bring all the people of God safely through the fire of judgment. By God's grace, Noah served as a type of the greater offspring and deliverer who was to come, pointing to Christ in his God-given righteousness while his failures and sins call our hearts to yearn for the greater offspring.

TODAY'S QUESTIONS

Noah was a man whose life was characterized by walking in obedience to God, yet he still fell into grievous sin. What kind of warning does Noah's sin offer us?

not to over indulge in things that could
lead to sin

How does today's passage point to the gospel?

it shows that His son's displayed care and
love to him

When you see someone's sin yourself or another person tells you about it, do you find your initial response to be more like that of Ham or of Shem and Japheth? What would it look like practically to imitate Shem and Japheth when you are tempted to gossip or hear gossip from someone else?

I use to want to go and spread it, but
since I got saved that has no longer
been the case.

Curses *and* Blessings

For further study: Leviticus 18, Galatians 3:26-29, Ephesians 2:11-22

Curses and Blessings

"The good news of the gospel declares that In Christ, those who were not part of God's original covenant people are brought into His family."

Ham sinned against his father by delighting in exposing Noah's sin. When Noah awoke from his drunken stupor, he discovered in his sobriety how Ham had ridiculed him. In response, Noah pronounced a curse on Ham's son Canaan and blessings on Shem and Japheth. The blessings and curses that Noah pronounced would only come true if God fulfilled them. The unfolding story of Scripture reveals that the words of Noah were actually oracles. God saw fit to prophesy through Noah about future events that would befall the descendants of Ham, Shem, and Japheth. These prophecies set the stage for the events that unfold in the remainder of the book of Genesis and the Old Testament as a whole.

Noah first pronounced a curse. He did not direct the curse at Ham but at the youngest of Ham's four sons, Canaan. Remember that the original audience of the book of Genesis consisted of the Israelites in the wilderness after God delivered them from slavery in Egypt. God had commanded them to drive out the people of Canaan from the land that God was calling the Israelites to inhabit. Their ears would have likely perked up upon hearing the mention of Canaan. The Canaanites were a people notorious for wickedness like that of Ham. Leviticus 18 describes their sinfulness as an example to avoid, repeatedly employing the word "nakedness" in the description. The original audience heard the story of Canaan as people who were direct witnesses to the tragic results of Ham's sin in his descendants. In directing the curse upon Canaan, Noah likely also saw the sinful behaviors of Ham already manifesting in Canaan. Canaan and his descendants would serve the descendants of Shem and Japheth.

Noah then turned to Shem with a blessing. The name Shem actually means name, and out of the three brothers, Shem is the only one whose oracle includes the covenant name for God, *Yahweh.* The fact that Noah refers to *Yahweh,* which is written as Lord or LORD in most Bible translations, as "the God of Shem" indicates that Shem was already in a covenant relationship with God. In fact, Shem's descendants would be the Israelites, God's covenant people. The blessing was not given directly to Shem but was directed at God. In light of Shem's covenant relationship with the Lord, Shem's greatest blessing was God Himself. It is through his line that the offspring would be born, and it is His descendants who are God's chosen people. He has a beautiful inheritance.

Noah then shifted from Shem to Japheth. The descendants of Japheth would be Indo-Europeans. Japheth also received a blessing correlating with his name. Japheth comes from the verb that means enlarge, and Noah appealed to God to extend, or enlarge, Japheth. Not only did Japheth's blessing include a growing family line but also that he would dwell in the tents of Shem. To dwell in Shem's tents would be to partake of his blessing. This blessing for Japheth was a prophecy that the descendants of Japheth would share in the covenant blessing of Shem—the blessing of salvation. They too would be part of the people of God. They would share in Japheth's inheritance.

> "In Christ there is not Greek and Jew, circumcision and uncircumcision, barbarian, Scythian, slave and free; but Christ is all and in all"
>
> Colossians 3:11

A look at Old Testament history and archaeology shows no evidence that the descendants of Japheth ever dwelt among the descendants of Shem. At first glance, it seems as if Japheth's blessing never came to fruition. However, the New Testament shows the fulfillment of this prophecy made long ago. The descendants of Japheth were not part of God's original covenant people. Those who were not Israelites were called Gentiles, and Japheth's line fits into this category. The good news of the gospel declares that In Christ, those who were not part of God's original covenant people are brought into His family. In Christ, Gentiles are adopted as God's children.

Some have interpreted the curse of Canaan to mean that an entire ethnic group was cursed because of Ham's sin, specifically those of African descent. This is a grievous misinterpretation of God's Word that should be entirely rejected. The descendants of Ham were not all African, nor did this curse apply to all of Ham's offspring. The Canaanites would later be conquered by the Israelites, sufficiently fulfilling this oracle. Now, in Christ, descendants of Ham are also brought into God's family. There is no distinction of family lineage or race. No skin color or language is exempt from the gospel of grace because, "In Christ there is not Greek and Jew, circumcision and uncircumcision, barbarian, Scythian, slave and free; but Christ is all and in all" (Colossians 3:11).

TODAY'S QUESTIONS

What does this passage reveal about the dangers of sin?

That bad things could happen if you do not turn away from sin.

What does today's passage reveal about God's grace?

That he wants to show grace, but you have to turn from sin. He continues to show grace even when we sin

How does today's passage point forward to a greater picture of God's plan for His people?

He wants to dwell w/ his people, if we turn from sin, he well show us his grace and we will be part of his plan.

The Table of Nations

The Table of Nations

"From a single line came every diverse culture on the globe.
All of humanity goes back to the same DNA."

Chapter 10 begins with another *toledot* and therefore a new section. This chapter of Genesis is known as the "Table of Nations," and it shows that the descendants of Shem, Ham, and Japheth spread abroad on the earth. When Noah and his family came off the ark, God commanded them to be fruitful and multiply and spread out upon the earth. This chapter is a picture of this command becoming a reality. It also lays the groundwork for the rest of the book of Genesis as it anticipates God's covenant with Abraham that is introduced in Genesis 12. God's promise to Abraham that all the nations of the world would be blessed directly corresponds to Genesis 10, which describes all the nations that God speaks about.

The chapter is structured in three parts, delineating the descendants of Japheth, then Ham, and finally Shem. Each section is separated by the refrain that the descendants spread out according to their "lands," "clans," "nations," and "languages." From these three men, and indeed from the one man Noah, came every nation of the world, every skin color in all their vibrant shades, and every unique language. From a single line came every diverse culture on the globe. All of humanity goes back to the same DNA. Paul the apostle pointed to this breathtaking reality when he addressed the racist Athenians in Acts 17. We all have the same blood pumping through our veins: the blood of Noah and the blood of Adam.

Moses begins with a brief overview of the posterity of Japheth. These people were Indo-European Gentiles. Moses quickly moves to the descendants of Ham, who were of particular interest to the original audience of Israelites, since it was Ham's descendants who became Israel's enemies. From Ham's son, Cush, came Nimrod, a powerful hunter reminiscent of the mighty men before the flood. The cities he established were notorious enemies of Israel. The empires of Babylon and Assyria would later exile the northern kingdom of Israel and the southern kingdom of Judah from their homes and included cities such as Nineveh, the city to which Jonah was sent. As should be expected from Noah's curse of Canaan, the names of the descendants of Ham's youngest son will be frequently repeated throughout the Old Testament as those who oppose Israel. These nations were idolatrous and full of all kinds of immorality and perversion.

Finally, Moses turns to Shem. This lineage was the family tree of the Israelites who were the original audience of Genesis. The rest of the book of Genesis will shift focus to this family line, and so its final position in the genealogy is fitting. Before mentioning Shem's own sons, the text points out that Shem is the father of all the sons of Eber, Shem's great grandson. The reason for this interjection is that the name Eber is where the term Hebrew comes from. From the Hebrew line would come Abraham, the one through whom God would carry on His covenant of grace. Through Abraham would come the promised offspring.

> By God's grace, He made a way for people from every land, every clan, every language, and every nation to be brought into the family of God.

While we may be tempted to skim quickly over genealogies like this one or skip them altogether, they appear in Scripture for a reason, and the author uses them intentionally to communicate specific truths. For the original audience, this list of names would have elicited all kinds of feelings about the nations they represent, from pride, to disgust and everything in between. Yet despite the differences between them, they will all be repeated in God's salvific covenant. The refrain of "lands," "clans," "nations," and "languages" describes all three family lines, and all of these nations will be included in the blessing of Abraham in the coming chapters. Through him, all the nations of the world will be blessed.

None of Noah's descendants were good enough to earn the grace of God. All of humanity, from Adam to Noah and all the way to us, is desperately wicked and depraved. The descendants of Shem, Ham, and Japheth were all in need of a savior. By God's grace, He made a way for people from every land, every clan, every language, and every nation to be brought into the family of God. The blood of Christ has made it so. Whether Jew or Gentile, may we join together in a resounding, "Thanks be to God!"

TODAY'S QUESTIONS

How does the structure of this passage emphasize God's chosen family line?

It shows where the chosen has come from.

How does the "Table of Nations" confront racism?

It tells us how every race, language was established.

What significance does this passage have for our own salvation today?

No matter the race, culture we all have the choice to accept God.

A People Dispersed

A People Dispersed

"They would build a city, and in the midst of it they would construct a tower so tall that its top would reach all the way to the heavens."

Immediately after the description of the descendants of Shem, Ham, and Japheth spreading throughout the world with different languages, chapter 11 begins with a statement that the entire earth spoke the same language. What may seem like a contradiction is actually an intentional disruption in the chronology of the narrative. Moses has just given a broad sweeping picture of Noah's family being fruitful and multiplying, spreading out across the earth, and filling it, and now he goes back to show how this reality came to pass. The story of Babel, or Babylon, shows that what may have seemed like simple obedience to God's command was actually much more complicated and sin-ridden. Chapter 10 anticipated the sinful nature of these events as it mentions Nimrod's connection to Babylon, whose very name means rebel, as well as mentioning that Peleg lived during the time when "the earth was divided."

Like the story of Noah, these 9 verses form a perfectly symmetrical chiasm. The first half shows man's attempt at glory and self-sufficiency, while the second half describes God thwarting their feeble attempts at divinity. The turning point is verse 5, when God comes down and intervenes. (See page 163).

The text describes people who migrated from the east and settled in a valley in the land of Shinar. They desired to make a name for themselves, and so they banded together and formulated a plan. They would build a city, and in the midst of it they would construct a tower so tall that its top would reach all the way to the heavens. They hoped that this city would give them a place to remain together, fearing the idea of being dispersed throughout the earth and losing their strength in numbers.

The sin displayed in this passage is twofold. First, the people are driven by pride. They desire their own glory rather than the glory of God's name. Their pursuit to make a name for themselves ominously recalls the primeval mighty men. They were called men of renown, or literally men of name. The efforts of the people to build a tower that reached up to the sky was an attempt to reach the place where God dwelled. They wanted to rise to God's level and perhaps even usurp Him. Like Eve's desire to be like God, they sought self-sufficiency in place of dependence on God. Second, their resolve to settle instead of being dispersed is in direct opposition to the command God gave to Noah to spread out over the earth and fill it. This pursuit is foolish in light of the variety of languages described in the "Table of Nations." They wanted the glory due to God for themselves, and they wanted life on their own terms.

This historical account also has a satirical tone. The project was doomed to fail from the beginning, and Moses emphasizes the folly of their pursuit as he describes their makeshift building materials. Instead of using stone and mortar, they made their own bricks. The fact that they build their tower out of baked bricks and bitumen mortar also indicates that it was likely a Mesopotamian ziggurat. Ziggurats were enormous, sacred towers that were described as the place where heaven meets earth. Babylon, or here Babel, called themselves Bab-ili, which means the gate of God, and their enormous ziggurat was known by many as the center of the world. Ziggurats were believed to be built by the gods, but just like Moses intentionally dismantled the belief that the sun and moon were gods in the creation account, he mocks the absurd belief that some other deities were responsible for this undertaking.

> They wanted the glory due to God for themselves, and they wanted life on their own terms.

All their arrogance and boasting is interrupted by verse 5: "and then God came down to look over the city and the tower that the humans were building." The irony of this statement is that the tower was supposed to reach the realm of the divine, but in reality, it was so far below God that He had to descend to reach it. He is high above the heavens, and He is transcendent over all. God is certainly all-knowing and all present and does not need to change positions for a better view, but the text uses anthropomorphic language to emphasize how much greater is the one true God than their feeble attempts at glory. The image is one of God stooping low to get a closer look at the relatively microscopic tower, just as a child on hands and knees with a magnifying glass to examine some tiny insect.

God saw what they were attempting and resolved to confuse their languages in order to disrupt their endeavor. God's statement that anything would be possible for them is not a statement of fear or threat but one of divine care for mankind. When banded together with one language, all the strength of humanity, although weak in God's eyes, would give man the dangerous illusion of self-sufficiency. They would cease to see their own need and fail to turn to God, all the while barreling toward death in their sin. In God's grace, He scattered the people abroad, fulfilling the command to fill the earth that man failed to fulfill on his own.

The sinful nature of man took what had the potential for good, a common language among all people, and used it to satisfy their own wicked desires. Zephaniah 3:9 prophecies about a time when all of God's people will have one pure speech to join together to call upon the name of the Lord and serve Him with one accord. At the Pentecost in Acts 2, those who received the Holy Spirit heard many languages as one, a foretaste of the final reality of all peoples coming together in one language when Christ returns. We will all worship Him with one voice, sinless and holy before Him.

The plight of Babel is the plight of so many of us. We fear obscurity, so we seek significance by making a name for ourselves. We believe that if we have the right job title or enough social media followers then our lives will matter. We seek money, power, position, and influence as our source of meaning, but seeking our own glory is a vain task. Even the most famous, the wealthiest, and the most influential among us are but specks of dust in comparison to the greatness of God. The fame and the fortune fades and decays, yet we can spend our entire lives seeking after things that will not last. It is vain to seek our own glory, but the glory of God is unending. Our lives matter when they are lived to glorify the Lord. We find meaning, not in ourselves but in Jesus Christ to whom we are united. Even the seemingly insignificant moments are eternally significant when done in service to the Lord. Let us spend our lives on what matters.

It is vain to seek our own glory, but the glory of God is unending.

—

Our lives matter when they are lived to glorify the Lord.

Man's attempt, God's intervention

A. The whole earth had one language. (11:1)

  B. They settled in Shinar. (1:2)

    C. "Come, let us make oven-fired bricks." (11:3)

      D. "Let us build..." (11:4)

        E. City and tower (11:4)

          F. "THE LORD CAME DOWN..." (11:5)

        E. City and tower (11:5)

      D. "Humans were building..." (11:5)

    C. "Come, let's go down there and confuse their language..." (11:7)

  B. God scattered them. (11:8)

A. God confused their language. (11:9)

TODAY'S QUESTIONS

What does the language of the text reveal about God in relation to man?

That he is not happy when man tries to glorify his own name, or life.

What was the motivation for the people of Babel in going against God's command to spread throughout the earth? Where do you see the tendency in your own life?

The motivation was to build a city to reach God, and to glorify their own name, Tendency in my own life is at work."

Read 1 Peter 1:13-25. In light of the fact that the things of this world are temporary and "all flesh is like grass," what are we called to spend our lives doing? How does this differ from what the people at Babel were seeking?

being obedient to God, People of Babel were seeking their own glory and not being obedient.

A Lineage of Grace

READ GENESIS 11:10-32

For further study: 1 Corinthians 1:18-31

A Lineage of Grace

"While the curse of sin continues, the hope of blessing swells with each new generation."

After God came down to the Tower of Babel and confused the languages of humanity, they spread abroad on the earth. All of humanity had joined together in sinful rebellion against God's authority, and now these fallen people were filling the entire world. At this point, Moses records another genealogy. This new *toledot* section is more concise, tracing the line of Shem, through whom God would continue His promise of the offspring. This passage is not just a list of names but a record of God's faithfulness against all odds.

The genealogy of Shem corresponds to the previous genealogy of Seth in Genesis 5. Both of these genealogies trace the continuation of God's promise to bring about the seed of the woman. Just as God carried on His promise through the faith of the one man, Noah, in Seth's genealogy, He preserved that same promise through the faith of the one man, Abram, in the genealogy of Shem. Both genealogies trace God's promise through ten generations. While the curse of sin continues, the hope of blessing swells with each new generation. This genealogy in chapter 11 ends with the three sons of Terah, paralleling the three sons of Noah that conclude the genealogy of Seth. Of these three sons, Abram is listed first even though he is not the oldest, just as Shem was listed first despite his age. The position of these two sons is not one of age but of prominence. It is through the line of Shem and Abram that God would fulfill His promise of salvation.

Peleg is at the center point of the genealogy pointing forward to the coming hope. Peleg was also mentioned in the "Table of Nations" with his brother Joktan, but Joktan is absent from this list. While Joktan's line led to the rebellion at Babel, it is through Peleg's offspring that God would continue His covenant. Ever since Genesis 3, God has been working to bring about the promised offspring through a family line. As the population of the world expands, the line of the offspring narrows according to God's sovereign plan.

God first promised that the offspring would come from Eve in Genesis 3, and with the birth of Cain, her heart was filled with hope that he would be the one to fulfill the promise. When Cain murdered Abel, she lost one son to death and the other to abhorrent sin. The hope of the offspring seemed lost, but God gave Eve another offspring named Seth. As his name suggests, he was indeed appointed by God to carry on the promise, but he was not the Promised One. Genesis 5 narrows into Seth's line, and after many generations one was born whose name means comfort. Noah's father hoped that he would be the one to bring relief from the painful toil of the sin-cursed ground. The earth became so infected by sin that every single human heart contained nothing but evil, and God's judgment was coming to decimate them all. But God remembered His promise, and out of all the inhabitants of the earth, God set His favor on one. By God's grace, Noah walked with God in righteousness, becoming His instrument to deliver eight people through the waters of judgment and preserve the human race and the line of the promised offspring.

> The line of the promised offspring is a lineage of grace, and the glory of redemption shines brighter for it.

Only Noah's three sons remained to carry on his lineage. Sin abounded in this fallen family, but God established His covenant with Shem. From Shem came the line of Eber, the namesake of the Hebrews who would be God's covenant people. The people of the earth rose up in rebellion against God as they built a tower to reach to heaven and were dispersed throughout the world, yet God saw fit to carry his promise through Eber's son, Peleg. From Peleg would come Abram, and through him, the promised offspring.

This family line was chosen by God to bring forth the Promised One. The names in this lineage do not represent the mightiest or those of great renown. It is not a line of firstborns or heroes in their own right. They are broken sinners, younger brothers, and all-around unlikely candidates to be ancestors of the Savior of the world, but God set His favor upon them. He called them by name and saw their weakness as an opportunity for His glory. The line of the promised offspring is a lineage of grace, and the glory of redemption shines brighter for it. In God's unending wisdom, He narrowed the promise to a single line so that redemption could come to all people. Years later, One would die so that the many could live.

The genealogy of chapter 11 ends with another unlikely choice to carry on the promise of God's grace. Abram was a man from a pagan nation whose barren wife disqualified him from carrying on the line of the Savior. Yet God chose this childless man to be the father of offspring more numerous than the stars. He chose Abram to carry on the line of the one offspring who would bring redemption where Adam brought death.

The end of chapter 11 marks the end of primeval history and the beginning of a new era. It is brimming with hope and anticipation of the One to whom all of history has been pointing. Through sin and suffering, death and destruction, God has been faithful to preserve His promise against all odds, and He will be faithful to see it through to the end.

Through sin and suffering, death and destruction, God has been faithful to preserve His promise against all odds.

ODAY'S QUESTIONS

What is surprising about the people in the lineage from Adam to Abram?
What does it reveal about the way God tends to work?

That he keeps his promises, that he will produce the one to bring salvation

As you think back over the events that took place in Genesis, where do you see evidence of God's sovereignty in carrying on the line of the promised offspring?

Have you ever experienced a time in your own life when it seemed like God would not come through? How does this section of Genesis encourage you in those situations?

yes, It encourages me, because if he promised something he will follow through with his promises

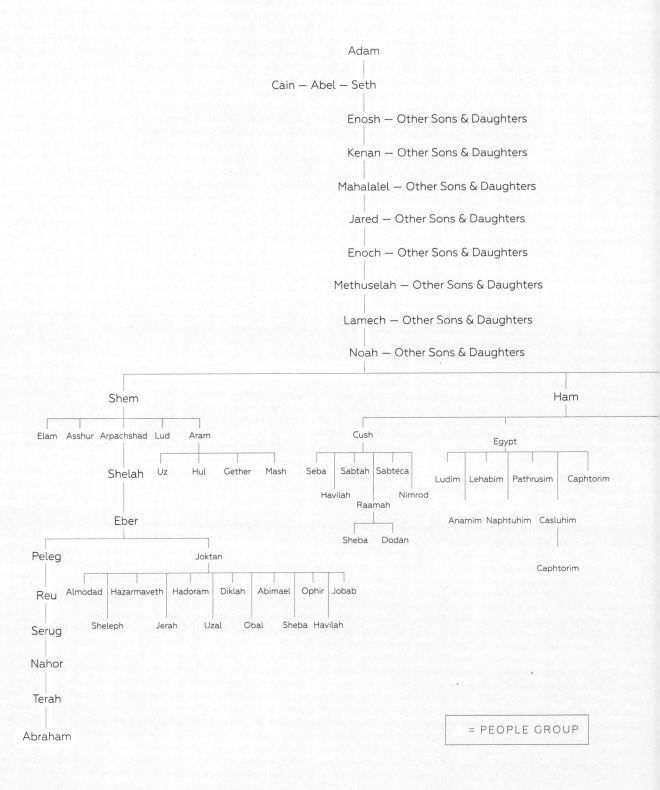

Adam

Cain — Abel — Seth

Enosh — Other Sons & Daughters

Kenan — Other Sons & Daughters

Mahalalel — Other Sons & Daughters

Jared — Other Sons & Daughters

Enoch — Other Sons & Daughters

Methuselah — Other Sons & Daughters

Lamech — Other Sons & Daughters

Noah — Other Sons & Daughters

Shem

Ham

Elam   Asshur   Arpachshad   Lud   Aram

Cush

Egypt

Shelah   Uz   Hul   Gether   Mash

Seba   Sabtah   Sabteca

Ludim   Lehabim   Pathrusim   Caphtorim

Havilah   Nimrod

Eber

Raamah

Anamim   Naphtuhim   Casluhim

Sheba   Dodan

Peleg

Joktan

Caphtorim

Reu

Almodad   Hazarmaveth   Hadoram   Diklah   Abimael   Ophir   Jobab

Serug

Sheleph   Jerah   Uzal   Obal   Sheba   Havilah

Nahor

Terah

Abraham

= PEOPLE GROUP

GENEALOGY

From Adam to Abraham

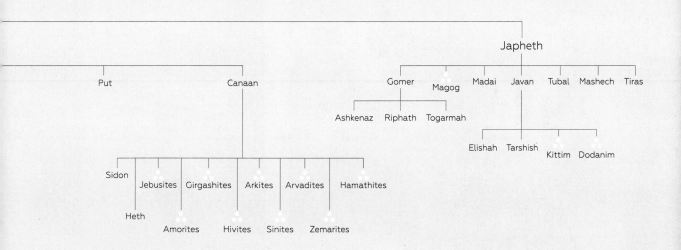

AND GOD SAID, "THIS IS THE SIGN OF THE COVENANT I AM MAKING BETWEEN ME AND YOU AND EVERY LIVING CREATURE WITH YOU, A COVENANT FOR ALL FUTURE GENERATIONS: I HAVE PLACED MY BOW IN THE CLOUDS, AND IT WILL BE A SIGN OF THE COVENANT BETWEEN ME AND THE EARTH.

Genesis 9:12-13

Paraphrase the passage from this week.

What did you observe from this week's text about God and His character?

What does this week's passage reveal about the condition of mankind and about yourself?

_____

_____

_____

_____

How does this passage point to the gospel?

_____

_____

_____

_____

How should you respond to this passage? What is the personal application?

_____

_____

_____

_____

What specific action steps can you take this week to apply this passage?

_____

_____

_____

_____

_____

*Thank you for studying
God's Word with us!*

CONNECT WITH US
@thedailygraceco
@kristinschmucker

CONTACT US
info@thedailygraceco.com

SHARE
#thedailygraceco
#lampandlight

VISIT US ONLINE
thedailygraceco.com

MORE DAILY GRACE
The Daily Grace App
Daily Grace Podcast